PINOLE
004

P9-DVJ-095

WITHDRAWN

A gift from:
Friends of the
Pinole Library

EXPLORING
ANCIENT
CIVILIZATIONS

8

Nineveh – Religion

CONTRA COSTA COUNTY LIBRARY

Marshall Cavendish
New York • London • Toronto • Sydney

3 1901 03607 2090

Marshall Cavendish
99 White Plains Road
Tarrytown, New York 10591-9001

www.marshallcavendish.com

© 2004 Marshall Cavendish Corporation

All rights reserved. No part of this book may be reproduced or utilized in any form or by any means, electronic or mechanical, including phocopying, recording, or by any information storage and retrieval system, without prior written permission from the publisher and the copyright holders.

Consultants: Daud Ali, School of Oriental and African Studies, University of London; Michael Brett, School of Oriental and African Studies, London; John Chinnery, School of Oriental and African Studies, London; Philip de Souza; Joann Fletcher; Anthony Green; Peter Groff, Department of Philosophy, Bucknell University; Mark Handley, History Department, University College London; Anders Karlsson, School of Oriental and African Studies, London; Alan Leslie, Glasgow University Archaeology Research Department; Michael E. Smith, Department of Anthropology, University at Albany; Matthew Spriggs, Head of School of Archaeology and Anthropology, Australian National University

Contributing authors: Richard Balkwill, Richard Burrows, Peter Chrisp, Richard Dargie, Steve Eddy, Clive Gifford, Jen Green, Peter Hicks, Robert Hull, Jonathan Ingoldby, Pat Levy, Steven Maddocks, John Malam, Saviour Pirotta, Stewart Ross, Sean Sheehan, Jane Shuter

WHITE-THOMSON PUBLISHING
Editors: Alex Woolf and Kelly Davis
Design: Derek Lee
Cartographer: Peter Bull Design
Picture Research: Glass Onion Pictures
Indexer: Fiona Barr

MARSHALL CAVENDISH
Editor: Thomas McCarthy
Editorial Director: Paul Bernabeo
Production Manager: Michael Esposito

Library of Congress Cataloging-in-Publication Data
Exploring ancient civilizations.
   p. cm.
Includes bibliographical references and indexes.
  ISBN 0-7614-7456-0 (set : alk. paper) -- ISBN 0-7614-7457-9 (v. 1 : alk. paper) -- ISBN 0-7614-7458-7 (v. 2 : alk. paper) -- ISBN 0-7614-7459-5 (v. 3 : alk. paper) -- ISBN 0-7614-7460-9 (v. 4 : alk. paper) -- ISBN 0-7614-7461-7 (v. 5 : alk. paper) -- ISBN 0-7614-7462-5 (v. 6 : alk. paper) -- ISBN 0-7614-7463-3 (v. 7 : alk. paper) -- ISBN 0-7614-7464-1 (v. 8 : alk. paper) -- ISBN 0-7614-7465-X (v. 9 : alk. paper) -- ISBN 0-7614-7466-8 (v. 10 : alk. paper) -- ISBN 0-7614-7467-6 (v. 11 : alk. paper)
  1. Civilization, Ancient--Encyclopedias.
  CB311.E97 2004
  930'.03--dc21

                            2003041224

ISBN 0-7614-7456-0 (set)
ISBN 0-7614-7464-1 (vol. 8)

Printed and bound in China

07 06 05 04 03 5 4 3 2 1

ILLUSTRATION CREDITS
AKG London: 576 (Robert O'Dea), 578 (Visioars), 580, 581 (Erich Lessing), 582 (Erich Lessing), 587 (John Hios), 597 (Erich Lessing), 599, 602 (Jean-Louis Nou), 618 (Erich Lessing), 622 (Erich Lessing), 624, 626, 633 (Erich Lessing), 638 (Erich Lessing).
Art Archive: 564, 620, 636.
Bridgeman Art Library: 569 (Heini Schneebeli), 573, 586, 588 (Lauros / Giraudon), 589 (Sally Greene), 592, 593, 598, 600, 601, 603, 605, 607 (Giraudon), 609, 610, 611, 614 (Ken Welsh), 615, 616, 617, 619, 621, 623, 625, 627 (Ken Welsh), 628 (Sean Sprague / Mexicolore), 629 (Index), 630, 631, 632, 634, 635, 636, 637 (Bonhams, London).
British Museum, London: 595.
Corbis: 570 (Tiziana and Gianni Baldizzone), 571 (Janet Wishnetsky).
Joann Fletcher: 590.
Hutchison Picture Library: 567 (Wilkinson).
Ann & Bury Peerless: 594.
University of Manchester: 604.
Werner Forman Archive: 565 (British Museum, London), 568 (W. Munsterberger Collection), 574 (Iraq Museum, Baghdad), 575, 577 (Museum für Völkerkunde, Berlin), 579 (National Museum of Anthropology, Mexico City), 584 (Anthropology Museum, Veracruz University, Jalapa, Mexico), 585, 608, 613 (Auckland Institute and Museum, New Zealand).

Contents

Nineveh

Nineveh, as it was known in the Bible (it was named Ninua by the Assyrians), is one of the oldest human settlements in the world. One of the two main mounds was used as long ago as the seventh millennium BCE. A legend, repeated in the Old Testament Book of Genesis, says that the hero Nimrod founded the city. By 4000 BCE Nineveh was a large town with trading links throughout Mesopotamia, and by 1800 BCE the city housed an important shrine to Ishtar, a principal goddess in Mesopotamian religion. The Assyrian king Sennacherib established Nineveh as his capital when he ascended the throne in 705 BCE.

Nineveh's Defenses

Nineveh was the center of a powerful military kingdom, and its arsenal (weapon store) was one of the largest buildings in the city. The outer city wall and its moat ran for 7.5 miles (12 km). Sennacherib called it "the wall that terrifies the enemy." It was pierced by fifteen gates, most of which were named after Assyrian gods, such as Ashur and Sin. The outer stone wall was fifty feet (15 m) high, with crenellated battlements. There were towers every ninety-eight feet (30 m). The inner wall was higher. Yet despite all these fortifications, Nineveh fell to the armies of the Medes and the Persians in 612 BCE.

Irrigation and Aqueducts

The land around Nineveh was fertile, but as the city grew, the rising population needed

Nineveh as it might have looked around the year 700 BCE. The palace complex is dominated by the main ziggurat (stepped pyramid).

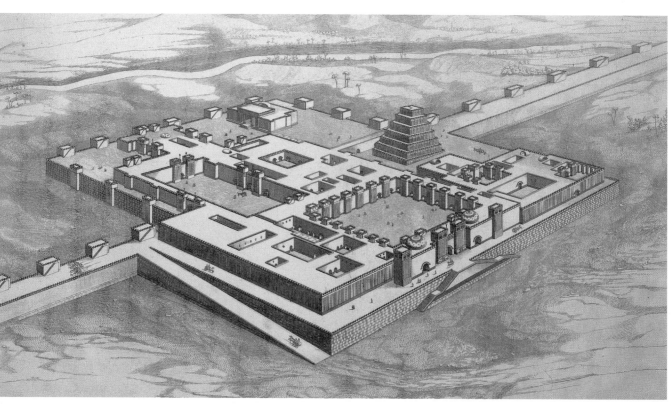

more water. Sennacherib ordered his engineers to build dams and canals to ensure that the city had an ample water supply.

Streams in the hills thirty miles (48 km) to the north were channeled toward the city by the aqueduct at Jerwan, one of the oldest known. The water enabled parks and orchards to flourish within the city walls. In Sennacherib's large garden grew plants sent from every part of his kingdom. One plant, called a "wool-bearing tree," was, scholars think, a cotton plant from India.

"Palace without a Rival"

In the seventh century BCE Nineveh was fabulously rich. Gifts poured in from the many peoples who feared Assyria. When the Assyrians conquered Egypt in 665 BCE, they carried some of its wealth back to Nineveh. Sennacherib's palace, the largest ever built to that date, was decorated with giant painted stone sculptures. His grandson Ashurbanipal added a library that contained over 1,500 inscribed clay tablets. The description "palace without a rival" comes from an Assyrian tablet of the seventh century BCE, found near the walls of Nineveh.

Survival

When the Medes and the Persians sacked Nineveh in 612 BCE, they looted the royal palaces and the city's shrines. Abandoned for many years, the city was reoccupied in the Hellenistic period around the year 250 BCE. Nineveh remained an important market town until about 500 CE, when it was eclipsed by nearby Mosul on the opposite bank of the Tigris.

NIMROD

According to the Bible, Nimrod, "the builder of kingdoms," founded many cities, including Nineveh and Calah (present-day Nimrud). His name survives in many place names in modern Iraq. The ancient Hebrews believed he was the great-grandson of Noah.

SEE ALSO

• Aqueducts • Ashurbanipal • Assyrians
• Ishtar • Palaces • Sennacherib

▲ This stone relief was sculpted to celebrate Ashurbanipal's victory over the Elamites in 653 BCE. It shows Ashurbanipal feasting with his queen while the head of the Elamite king, Teumman, hangs from the tree on the left.

Nok Culture

Nok culture flourished in present-day central Nigeria, in West Africa, during the African Iron Age. The people and their culture are named after the small village of Nok, where some pottery figures were found in the late 1920s and early 1930s. It was not archaeologists but tin miners working in the area who accidentally discovered the first evidence of the ancient Nok civilization.

The Iron Age Nok culture developed between about 500 BCE and 200 CE. Until Nok culture was firmly identified in 1943 by Bernard Fagg, a British archaeologist, there had been only occasional finds of Stone Age tools and artifacts in western Africa. The wealth of finds from the Nok area, about three hundred miles (480 km) in width and two hundred miles (320 km) from north to south, indicates that the Nok people may have been among the first to have an organized social life in this part of Africa. This advanced social organization may be partly due to the fact that they were the first to manufacture iron south of the Sahara Desert, although stone tools and implements have also been found.

Very little is known about Nok culture because it had no form of writing and the circumstances surrounding the decline of Nok remain unknown. The people of Nok were farmers who also hunted and gathered, and they probably lived in huts made from clay.

Iron Makers

The technology of iron making reached the coast of North Africa from western Asia, which lay farther east in the Mediterranean. From North Africa the new knowledge could have gradually spread to West Africa across the Sahara Desert. It is also possible that the new technology spread westward from the kingdom of Kush in present-day Sudan. Iron smelting was an important activity in the Kush capital of Meroe, which flourished after 500 BCE. However, the technique may have been an independent invention by the people of Nok and perhaps by the first Bantu people of East Africa. By 200 BCE the knowledge of iron making that the Nok people possessed was widespread across Africa south of the Sahara.

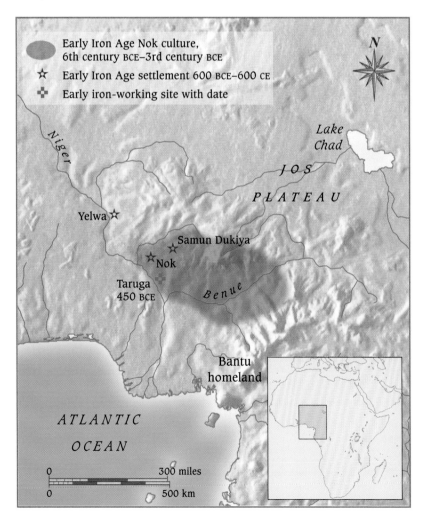

▼ The area in which Nok terra-cotta heads, dating from 500 BCE to 200 CE, were found.

Early Iron Age Nok culture, 6th century BCE–3rd century BCE

☆ Early Iron Age settlement 600 BCE–600 CE

✚ Early iron-working site with date

Niger

Lake Chad

JOS PLATEAU

Yelwa ☆

☆ Samun Dukiya
☆ Nok
Taruga 450 BCE

Benue

Bantu homeland

ATLANTIC OCEAN

N

0   300 miles
0   500 km

IRON-SMELTING TECHNOLOGY

The ability to make tools and weapons out of iron, instead of stone or bronze, was an important advance for all ancient civilizations. Iron is a hard, strong metal that occurs naturally in the ground in the form of iron ore. Pure iron is separated from iron ore by a process known as smelting, whereby the ore is heated to so high a temperature that the iron melts. The earliest iron-smelting furnace found in Africa south of the Sahara is from Nok. It dates from around 450 BCE, though before this time it is very likely that smelting was carried out in simple trenches dug in the ground. By using a furnace that could be fanned with a bellows to reach the required temperature of 2,012° F (1,100° C), the Nok people were able to produce a better quality of iron. The furnaces were made from clay, and clay piping was added to provide draughts that helped maintain the extremely high temperature needed for smelting.

NOK CULTURE

c. 1000 BCE

Iron-making technology reaches Africa.

800 BCE–250 CE

Kingdom of Kush flourishes.

500 BCE–250 CE

Nok culture flourishes.

c. 450 BCE

Date of earliest iron-smelting furnace found at Taruga, in the region of Nok.

◀ A craftswoman in Cameroon extracts iron from iron ore using techniques that have changed little since the ancient Nok culture flourished in nearby Nigeria.

Nok Sculptures

The Nok artistic tradition of sculpting animal and human figures influenced all western Africa. Nok sculptors probably first used wood and progressed to clay when methods of firing—the heating process that hardens clay—were perfected. Nok people may have fired clay in much the same way as it is still being fired in parts of western Africa, by covering pieces of clay with grass, twigs, and leaves that are then burned for about two hours.

The sculpted figures, ranging in size from one inch (2.5 cm) to life-size, reveal technical mastery and a mature style. The figures were first shaped from a coarse-grained clay and then covered with slip, a fine clay mixed with water, to produce a smooth, glossy surface. Mostly heads have been uncovered, perhaps because only these more solid and resistant parts remained intact under the ground.

Nok artists carved human features so as to create a dramatic and emotional impact, rather than a realistic portrait. The eyes in Nok life-size heads are often hollowed-out spaces, triangular or half circular in shape, with eyebrows formed by a segment of a circle. Ears—and sometimes nostrils and lips—are pierced, and the lips are usually curled. Finally, great attention is paid to personal adornments. The overall effect is often startling.

The Nok artists who sculpted terra-cotta figures achieved a remarkable expressiveness, and their work may well have influenced the later artistic achievements of the Yoruba people. By 900 CE the Iron Age culture of the Ife kingdom of the Yoruba people had developed in an area four hundred miles (640 km) to the southwest. Nok art may also have influenced the artistic tradition that later emerged at Benin in West Africa.

The sculpted figures of Nok are thought to have been used for ritual or religious purposes, and it has been suggested that there may have been a rule in Nok culture that forbade the exact portrayal of human figures. Some of the figures have dome-shaped bases, an indication that they were once attached to parts of shrines or royal ancestral tombs.

▼ Nok terra-cotta heads typically have holes marking the positions of the eye sockets and the nostrils.

NOK FIGURINES

The Nok sculpted many human figures that have a very stylized appearance, especially the larger, almost life-size ones. The faces are very long, with large, rounded foreheads and small chins. The heads are frequently distorted into a conelike or tubular shape and have decorative hairstyles, often braided or composed of beautifully arranged buns or tresses. Some of these hairstyles may still be seen among people living in the region. Some of the clay figures wear elaborate headgear; others are adorned with expertly sculpted pearl jewelry.

The hollow figurines were finely shaped in clay and fired in furnaces. Some of these furnaces have been excavated in the Nok area, and they indicate the settled and prosperous nature of Nok culture.

The attention paid to personal adornment in Nok clay figurines and the elegant details of different hairstyles suggest an advanced culture able to concern itself with nonessential aspects of living. It is also interesting that Nok artists carved human figures and heads with physical abnormalities and deformities, although the reason they did so is not clear.

▼ The face of this Nok terra-cotta figurine, part human and part bird, has the typical large, round forehead and narrow chin.

SEE ALSO
• Art • Bantu Culture • Pottery

Nomadism

The word *nomad* comes from the Greek *nomados*, meaning "roving for pasture." Nomadism is a way of life in which people move on to find new grasslands for their livestock at different times of year. Historically there have been many nomadic tribes in central Asia, Arabia, North Africa, and the area of northern Europe and Asia to the south of the Arctic Circle. The people in these regions became nomads partly because the areas they came from were too dry, too cold, too high, or too steep for them to practice settled agriculture.

▼ Camels have been used by nomads for thousands of years. The camel has tremendous stamina, can carry heavy equipment across difficult desert terrain with ease, and can survive for many days without water.

Nomads use the resources of one area and, when their animals exhaust the grazing and water, move on to another area. In the deserts of Arabia the nomads camp near oases during the intense heat of the summer months. Later, after the rains fall, they move their herds of goats into the desert and head for their familiar pasture.

Steppe Nomads

The steppe nomads of Eurasia were an ancient nomadic civilization that existed in the first millennium BCE. The steppes are a huge belt of grassland that stretches from European Russia to Manchuria in China. As this area was much too dry for agriculture, by 1000 BCE the economy was based on the rearing of cattle, sheep, and horses. Horse riding was clearly very important, because the remains of horses have been found in some impressive burial mounds. At Kostromskaya in the Caucasus, no fewer than twenty-two horses were buried along with thirteen humans, probably the dead chieftain's servants. A shield, spears, arrows, and a leather quiver dating back to the sixth or seventh century BCE were found among the grave contents.

According to writers from China, Persia, and Greece, the steppe nomads lived in tribes led by warrior chiefs. The steppe

SHELTER

*S*helter has always been very important for nomadic people, and the form it takes depends on a number of factors—the type of animal grazed, terrain, and climate. Shelter has to be portable but still able to withstand extremes of weather. The tent is the most common form of nomadic shelter. It is usually made of animal skins stitched together and stretched over tent poles and fastened by ropes and pegs. In areas of little vegetation, the wooden poles are valuable and are carried with the skins. The nomads of the Sahara made their tents from black goat's hair, as they had a plentiful supply from the herds they kept. The steppe nomads used a tent design unchanged for thousands of years, known as the ger. It had light, collapsible wooden walls and a roof covered with layers of sheepskin.

tribesmen fought on horseback with the Hunnish reflex bow, an incredibly powerful weapon found in steppe burials along with swords and lances. The Greek historian Herodotus (c. 484–c. 420 BCE) described how the nomads of the Ukraine scalped their enemies and kept the hair as war trophies.

In the ancient world nomadism was common. However, changes in the environment, including long periods of drought and the spread of dry, desert land beginning in about 4000 BCE, made life increasingly difficult for nomads. Slowly their numbers dwindled. Nomadism is now practiced by only a few small groups in Africa, Arabia, and Asia.

▶ *For life on the move, it is essential that any equipment be easy to dismantle and carry. These women, on the steppes of Kyrgyzstan, are weaving cloth on a portable loom in front of their yurt (a wooden-framed tent).*

SEE ALSO
• Farming

Nubians

Nubia was an ancient African kingdom south of Egypt, in what is now the Republic of Sudan. The origins of Nubian civilization go back to the late Stone Age (5000 BCE). The first Nubian kings appeared at the same time as the first Egyptian pharaohs (3000–2000 BCE), but Nubia outlasted the Egyptian empire by 1,500 years.

▼ *Nubia and Egypt.*

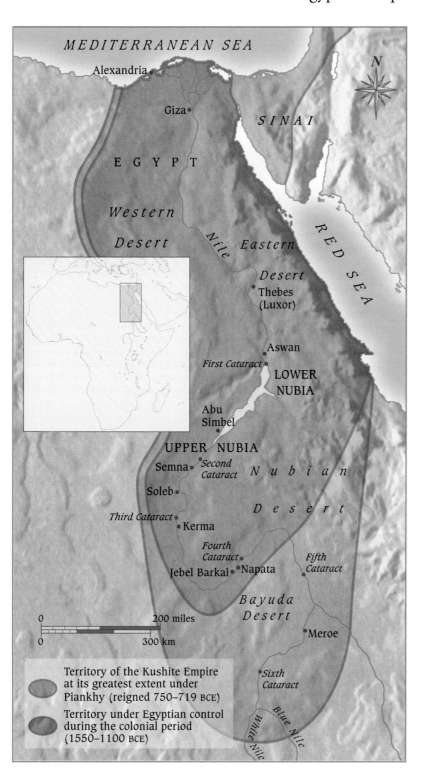

MEDITERRANEAN SEA

Alexandria

Giza

SINAI

EGYPT

Western
Desert

Nile

Eastern
Desert

RED SEA

Thebes
(Luxor)

Aswan

First Cataract

LOWER
NUBIA

Abu
Simbel

UPPER NUBIA

Semna Second
Cataract

Nubian

Soleb

Desert

Third Cataract

Kerma

Fourth
Cataract

Fifth
Cataract

Jebel Barkal Napata

Bayuda
Desert

Meroe

0   200 miles

0   300 km

Sixth
Cataract

White Nile

Blue Nile

Territory of the Kushite Empire
at its greatest extent under
Piankhy (reigned 750–719 BCE)

Territory under Egyptian control
during the colonial period
(1550–1100 BCE)

The Nubians first wrote in Egyptian hieroglyphs; they did not write down their own language until very late, and those writings remain undeciphered. However, archaeologists have found a great many Nubian artifacts that reveal much about the Nubian way of life.

Early History

Starting sometime around 4500 BCE, first in southern and then in northern Nubia, people scattered along the Nile River began to plant crops and keep animals. In about 3500 BCE a culture known as the A-Group appeared in Lower (northern) Nubia. Graves from this period suggest that Nubian society was divided into two classes and perhaps was ruled by kings. The graves of the rich ruling class are filled with luxurious items; the poor farmers, unsurprisingly, had simpler graves.

In about 3100 BCE Egypt united under the first pharaohs, and the A-Group flourished for a while under Egyptian influence before its people were attacked and conquered. In about 2300 BCE, however, Egypt withdrew, and another wealthy Nubian culture (the C-Group) subsequently emerged in Lower Nubia.

However, between 1950 and 1850 BCE the Twelfth Dynasty of Egyptian pharaohs again conquered Lower Nubia and seized control of Nubian trade. These pharaohs also built eleven massive fortresses along the Nile to defend their territory.

NUBIANS

3500–2900 BCE

A-Group culture flourishes in Lower, or northern, Nubia.

2500–2200 BCE

The Kingdom of Yam flourishes in Upper, or southern, Nubia.

2300–1500 BCE

C-Group culture flourishes in Lower Nubia.

1700–1550 BCE

The kingdom of Kerma flourishes in Upper Nubia.

1550–1100 BCE

The whole of Nubia is ruled by Egypt (a time known as the colonial period).

900 BCE

The kingdom of Kush emerges, first at Napata and then at Meroe.

350 CE

Meroe is sacked by the Ethiopian kingdom of Axum.

540 CE

Christian period begins.

▲ This relief from Amarna, Egypt, shows a Nubian soldier. By the end of the Egyptian Old Kingdom (2181 BCE), the Egyptian army was composed largely of Nubian mercenaries, who would ultimately marry Egyptian women and settle in Egypt.

Nubia and Egypt

Nubia's fortunes were always closely linked to those of Egypt, and there were several periods when Egypt controlled northern Nubia. From 1550 to 1100 BCE (the colonial period), the whole of Nubia was governed by Egypt.

Egyptian writers referred to Nubia as "hateful Kush," while Egyptian artists frequently depicted Nubians as chained prisoners. Nubians were sometimes painted on the soles of the pharaoh's sandals or on the floors of temples so that they would be stepped on.

Yet for long periods of their history, the two civilizations cooperated with each other. Nubian soldiers fought in Egyptian armies, and Nubian archers were famed for their skill. One of the ancient Egyptian names for Nubia was Ta-Seti, which means "land of the bow."

SENUSTRIS III, WHO RULED ABOUT 1850 BCE, WAS A PHARAOH OF THE EGYPTIAN MIDDLE KINGDOM. THE NUBIANS, HE SAID,

. . . are not people one respects. They are cowardly wretches. . . . I have captured their women, I have carried off their dependents, gone to their wells, killed their cattle, cut down their grain and set it afire. As my father lives for me, I speak the truth! There is no boasting in what comes out of my mouth.

FROM A STELA FOUND AT SEMNA,
ONE OF ELEVEN FORTRESSES BUILT TO DEFEND THE NILE

▶ During their long and
turbulent shared history,
Nubia and Egypt were
often bitter enemies.
Egypt's fear and hatred of
its neighbor to the south
is a subject of much
Egyptian art, such as this
eighth-century-BCE ivory
inlay of a lioness killing a
Nubian, found in
Phoenicia, at that time an
Egyptian colony.

During the colonial period the most privileged young Nubians were sent to the Egyptian palaces to be educated, especially in matters of law, religion, trade, and morality. These Egyptianized Nubians would usually return as governors of Nubia, bringing Egyptian customs back with them. There is further evidence of the close relationship of the two civilizations in the many tomb paintings showing Egyptian pharaohs with darker-skinned Nubian wives.

Trade

The Nile was an essential trade route. It started far to the south, wound its way through Nubia, and continued up through Egypt to the Mediterranean. The Egyptians wanted access to goods from central Africa, such as animal skins, ivory, ebony, and gold. These goods came from beyond Nubia, an area known by Egyptians as the "land of the horizon dwellers." The Nubian civilizations thrived by controlling the trade of these goods.

Royal Burial

The earliest Nubian graves date back to 5000 BCE (the late Stone Age); their burial customs changed very little until the Christian era, in the sixth century CE. Deep holes were dug in the ground. Sometimes two or three chambers were built in these holes and lavishly decorated with paintings and inscriptions. The body was placed inside, often on a bed. The hole was filled in with sand and covered with an earthen mound. The most important kings had huge mounds, sometimes 328 feet (100 m) across.

Nubians were buried with so-called grave goods, objects needed to help them in their journey in the afterlife, such as food and drink, weapons, and clothing. These grave goods tell historians a great deal about Nubian society at the time of burial. Sometimes members of the king's household, such as servants, relatives, horses, and pet dogs, would be sacrificed and buried with the king. Being sacrificed was considered an honorable death.

The Kingdoms of Yam and Kerma and the Colonial Period

In Upper Nubia the kingdom of Yam flourished from 2500 to 2200 BCE. Its successor was the kingdom of Kerma, whose capital, the city of Kerma, was not only the first Nubian city but also a very large and wealthy city. In 1700 BCE the Egyptians withdrew from northern Nubia to fight off invaders in the north of Egypt, and the kings of Kerma moved in. However, between 1550 and 1479 BCE, with the invaders finally defeated, the pharaohs swept southward again and destroyed Kerma and took control of both Lower and Upper Nubia. The whole of Nubia, under the name of Kush, remained part of Egypt for four hundred years.

▶ This pyramid at Meroe dates from Nubia's Meroitic period (c. 300 BCE–c. 300 CE). Meroitic kings were buried with their sacrificed servants and sometimes with comrades and friends (sacrificial death was considered to be honorable).

RELIGION

The Nile in Lower Nubia flowed through the harsh, rocky desert. During the day the temperatures were fierce, with strong dry winds, while at night it was freezing. In Nubian religion the brutal summer heat was associated with the flaming breath of the lioness god Sekhmet, who was trying to destroy mankind. The Nubians believed that if they did not worship Sekhmet, the heat would kill them. The New Year was under the control of Tefnut, the god of moisture and floods, another lioness. She also had to be appeased with rituals, because if the floods were too heavy the land would be swamped and no crops would grow. Every fall the Nubians prayed that the god Shu would bring cooling winds and carry Tefnut away to Egypt with him.

This temple at Abu Simbel, Lower Nubia, was built under the Egyptian pharaoh Ramses II (1290–1224 BCE) to glorify his divine aspect (or ka) and to impress the subject Nubians with his overwhelming power.

The Kingdom of Kush

From 1100 BCE, as Egypt slipped into decline, the powerful kingdom of Kush emerged in Nubia. In 728 BCE King Piankhy marched north, and for sixty-five years the whole of Egypt was under Kushite rule. The kings built pyramids, restored the ancient temples, and used the Egyptian language. From 900 BCE their capital was at Napata, but in about 450 BCE they moved south to Meroe, near modern Khartoum.

PIANKHY

Piankhy, king of the Kushites from 750 to 719 BCE, was intelligent, devout, and wise. He spent the first two decades of his reign at Napata before marching north and defeating the Egyptian armies of Tefnakht. As a result, the kingdom of Kush extended all the way to the Mediterranean. Piankhy named himself pharaoh and is considered the founder of the Twenty-fifth Dynasty. After his triumph he returned to his homeland and lived in Nubia.

In Meroe, for the first time, Nubians started writing down their own language, known as Meroitic.

The Coming of Christianity

The Kushites defended Nubia from the various conquerors of Egypt—Assyrians, Greeks, Romans, and Arabs. They continued to control the trade of goods up the Nile. However, in the fourth century CE Meroe was sacked by the Christian king of Axum in Ethiopia. Two hundred years later three new Nubian kingdoms emerged: Nobatia in Lower Nubia; Makuria in the region of Napata; and Alodia in the region of Meroe. In the mid-sixth century they were converted to Christianity by missionaries sent by the Byzantine emperor Justinian and the empress Theodora.

SEE ALSO
- Amenhotep III • Amun • Book of the Dead
- Egypt • Egyptian Mythology • Pyramids
- Ramses II • Thebes • Tutankhamen
- Valley of the Kings

Numbers

All ancient peoples used numbers. Even the Incas in South America, who had not developed any written language, counted by making knots in colored cords called quipus. Ancient number systems were often based on ten, the number of fingers a person had to count with. Such a system is called a decimal system. The Chinese, who had a decimal system from about 400 BCE, counted with marked bamboo rods.

India and Mesopotamia

There is evidence that the Egyptians were using ten symbols to express every possible number as early as 3000 BCE, and that ancient Indian civilizations were using a decimal system by around 2500 BCE.

In Mesopotamia the Akkadians seem to have used the abacus for counting. An existing clay tablet suggests that the Babylonians knew some geometry, as did the Egyptians, who also constructed tables to help with their calculations. For example, one tablet from about 2000 BCE gives the squares of all numbers up to fifty-nine.

Base Number Systems

A key invention of ancient civilizations was the idea of having a base when using numbers. The Egyptians, like the Chinese and others, had a decimal, or base ten, system, while the Maya used twenty as a base and the Babylonians sixty.

A number system with a base has several advantages over one without. Base systems handle large numbers simply, without too many symbols. For example, the Babylonians made vertical cuneiform marks for numbers one to nine. (The number nine was represented by nine marks clustered in a square.) For tens, they made horizontal marks, so ten to fifty-nine were horizontal and vertical strokes together. Sixty was one vertical mark again. Sixty-two was therefore a single vertical, a gap, and then two horizontals.

▶ *Inca mathematicians, known as Keepers of the Quipu, tied knots in pieces of string (quipus) to record numerical and information, such as numbers of llamas and quantites of agricultural produce.*

▶ *Known as the Rhind papyrus, this Egyptian document is one of the oldest surviving examples of ancient mathematics. Dating from around 1550 BCE, it was copied from an original dating from about 350 years earlier.*

The advanced aspect of a base system is "positional dependence." In modern counting, depending on its position, the number one can mean one or ten or a hundred or more. In the same way the value of a cuneiform mark depended on its position, with the farthest right-hand position representing the lowest value.

Representing Numbers

The Egyptians were using hieroglyphs for numbers as far back as about 3250 BCE. The early Chinese had separate written characters for the numbers one to nine, as well as for ten and for one thousand, and the characters were positioned from left to right. The Roman number system, simple but not very practical, was based on shapes formed when counting with fingers.

The Maya, who were skilled mathematicians, represented numbers according to two methods. One was a bar and dot arrangement, in which each bar represented five and each dot one, the dot perhaps derived from using cocoa beans or pebbles as currency. (The word *calculation* comes from the Latin *calcule*, which means "pebble.") A second Maya system represented different numbers by means of abstract heads drawn in various ways.

Numbers and the Annual Calendar

The Babylonians and the Maya were highly skilled in both numbers and astronomy. The Maya calculated the length of the year, with remarkable precision, at 365.242 days. The Babylonian year, however, was 360 days, divided into twelve months of thirty days each. This calculation made a total that was five and a quarter days shorter than the true year of 365.25 days, so the Babylonians needed to add an extra month every six years in order to catch up. The Babylonians may also have been the first civilization to divide hours into sixty minutes. The Egyptians were the first to divide the year into 365 days, which they further divided into thirty-six ten-day weeks, with the five remaining days being celebrated as the birthdays of the gods.

NUMBERS, MAGIC, AND RELIGION

Numbers generally had many more religious and magical meanings in early civilizations than they have now. In ancient times as now, thirteen was considered an unlucky number. In several stories from western Asia, heroes shrink from opening the thirteenth door. However, for the Maya, who believed that there were thirteen layers in the heavens, thirteen was a good number. Certain Mayan numbers represented central aspects of their world. For instance, four stood for the sun god, eight the maize god, one the beginning, and nine the levels of the underworld.

In some civilizations eight was a very positive number, with connections to the idea of heaven. For instance, the Chinese had eight pillars of heaven. For the ancient Greek mathematicians Pythagoras and Aristotle and their followers, the eighth sphere of "fixed stars" was located beyond the seven spheres of the moving, "unreliable" planets.

▼ The carved animals and gods on this Mayan limestone sculpture combine to make a date that corresponds to February 11, 526 CE.

Numbers, Weights, and Measures

The Egyptians were using bronze and stone weights as early as 3500 BCE. By 2500 BCE there was also a standardized system of weights and measures in Sumer in Mesopotamia. Perhaps Babylonian numbers were somehow devised to make trading straightforward, or it may be that an efficient number system helped Babylonian trading and industry to develop. Some tablets have been found inscribed with calculations as to how many workers would be needed to dig a canal in a certain number of days.

◄ *This 1547 woodcut shows Archimedes in his bath, noting for the first time in history how an object in water—himself—loses weight equal in amount to the weight of water it displaces.*

The Invention of Zero

Many ancient civilizations, including the Romans, lacked zero. This vital numeral appeared only gradually. In the Babylonian area, around 400 BCE, two wedge-shaped symbols were used to distinguish between, for instance, 2016 and 216. Three hooks were used for zero at Kish in Mesopotamia in about 700 BCE. The Chinese left a space. Greek astronomers were the first to use an *O* as zero. The Maya represented zero first by a cross and later by an empty oyster.

SEE ALSO

- Akkadians • Astronomy • Babylon • China
- Egypt • Indus Valley • Maya • Mesopotamia
- Science • Weights and Measures

ARCHIMEDES *287–212 BCE*

Archimedes was one of the greatest mathematicians and inventors of all time. He was born in the Greek colony of Syracuse, Sicily, and also died there, killed while working by a Roman soldier who did not know who he was.

Archimedes invented the screw, an invaluable piece of technology that is still widely used, in Alexandria. Archimedes's screw lifts water up a closed tube by the rotation of a screw device inside the tube. For Hieron, king of Syracuse, he is said to have invented war machines, including the first catapult, remarkable lever systems, and a small planetarium (a working model of the stars and planets that demonstrates their movement). Archimedes wrote books about geometry, arithmetic, and mechanics. His famous principle states that an object immersed in water loses weight equal to the weight of the water it displaces.

The Greek number system was ill-equipped to deal with very large quantites, so Archimedes devised a system for writing huge numbers—large enough to count the number of grains of sand in the universe, he said.

Odysseus

Odysseus, king of the island of Ithaca, was a mythical hero of ancient Greece, best known for his roles in two epic poems, the *Iliad* and the *Odyssey*. Although a great fighter, Odysseus became renowned for his cunning, diplomacy, and persuasiveness. He was a new kind of hero, intelligent as well as strong and brave. It was fitting that he was said to be a favorite of Athena, goddess of wisdom and war.

The Trojan War

Odysseus tried to avoid leaving his native Ithaca for the Trojan War by pretending to be mad. However, once he had been found out, he led twelve ships to Troy and showed cleverness and courage throughout the war. When Achilles, one of the Greek heroes, died, Odysseus and another Greek warrior, Ajax, argued over who should get his armor. When it was granted to Odysseus, Ajax went mad and killed himself. Odysseus showed his compassion by persuading the Greeks to give Ajax a proper funeral. Later Odysseus showed typical cleverness in devising the Trojan horse, in which the Greeks smuggled themselves into Troy.

The Journey Home

According to the *Odyssey*, Odysseus and his men had many adventures on their journey home. They fought the warlike Ciconians and resisted giving in to drugged sleep with the Lotus-eaters. Next Odysseus and some of his men were trapped in the cave of a man-eating one-eyed monster, the Cyclops, but Odysseus blinded the Cyclops and found a way to escape. On another island the generous Aeolus gave Odysseus four winds in a bag to help him sail home, but Odysseus's men let them out, and they were swept away in a storm.

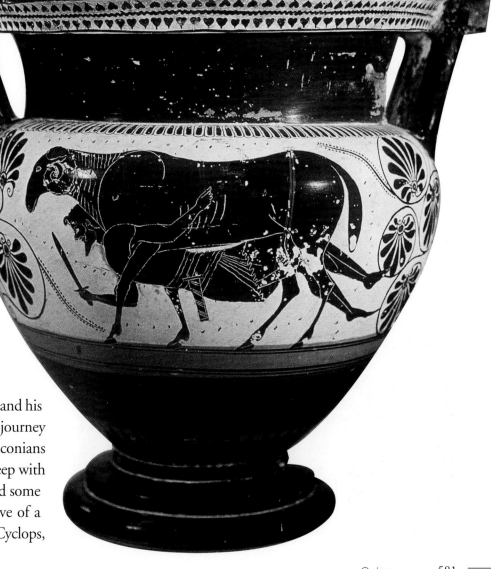

▼ This early-sixth-century-BCE Greek vase shows Odysseus escaping from the cave of the Cyclops concealed beneath one of the Cyclops's rams.

Odysseus and his men encountered more man-eating giants and then the witch Circe, who turned them into pigs. Eventually restored to human form, they sailed on to Hades, where Odysseus talked to dead heroes. Next came twin threats: the six-headed monster Scylla and the whirlpool Charybdis. After this adventure the crew was killed by a storm for angering the sun god Helios. Odysseus survived but was held captive by the nymph Calypso for seven years. Finally, he returned to Ithaca, where he and his son, Telemachus, fought and killed a crowd of rowdy suitors who wanted to marry his wife, Penelope.

▼ *Odysseus, disguised as an old man by the goddess Athena, speaks to his grieving wife, Penelope, who does not recognize him.*

ODYSSEUS DESCRIBES HIS GRIEF FOR HIS CREW AS THEY ARE DEVOURED BY THE MONSTER SCYLLA:

As I looked into the swift ship to find my men, I saw their feet and hands as they were lifted on high, crying aloud in agony, and calling me by my name for the last time. Just as when a fisherman on a headland lets down his baits on a long rod to snare the little fish below, casting an ox horn into the deep, and as he catches each fish and flings it writhing ashore, so were my men carried writhing up to the cliff. There Scylla devoured them shrieking in her jaws, stretching out their hands to me in their death-struggle. This was the saddest thing I have seen in all my journeys searching out the paths of the sea.

HOMER, ODYSSEY, BOOK 13

SEE ALSO

• Agamemnon • Athena • Greek Mythology
• Iliad and Odyssey
• Mycenaean Civilization • Mythology
• Troy • Zeus

Olmecs

The Olmecs lived on the Gulf Coast of Mexico. Historians estimate that La Venta, a center of Olmec civilization, was established around 1000 BCE; Olmec civilization is thus far older than the Maya civilization that followed. The area where the Olmecs lived was small, and few sites have survived. Nevertheless, the Olmecs may have been the founders of much early Mesoamerican culture.

Where the Olmecs Lived

The Olmec people lived in hot and humid lowlands along the coast of the Mexican Gulf. The surviving sites are La Venta island, which lies on the Tonalá River, and San Lorenzo on the Coatzacoalcos River, about thirty-seven miles (60 km) from La Venta. In this region the Olmec people began to establish small communities around 1500 BCE. There is some evidence that they traded in obsidian (a volcanic glass that could be worked to make tool blades), which they imported from the highlands, and building materials, such as stone. The Olmecs also made carved jade and ceramic clay figures, which they traded in Oaxaca and Morelos.

At San Lorenzo people built homes and ceremonial structures on raised platforms of stones above the river level. They had courtyards and a ball court. Several huge carved heads, for which the Olmecs are famous, are found at San Lorenzo, as well as at nearby La Venta and at Tres Zapotes.

San Lorenzo was unfinished, and it declined between 900 and 700 BCE. Some of the heads were defaced, perhaps by the Olmecs themselves. At the same time La Venta grew in size and importance from about 1000 BCE onward. Then, like San Lorenzo, it went into decline. By 300 BCE the Maya had established their communities, and Olmec culture ceased to be separate and distinct.

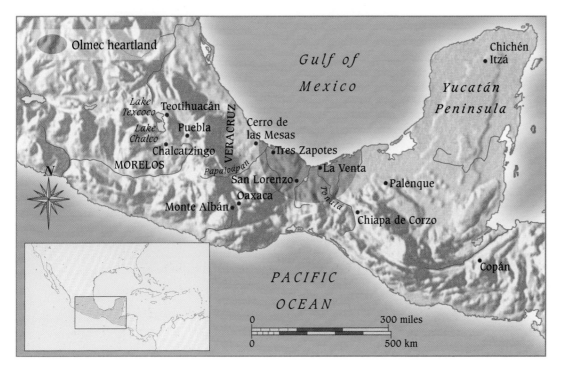

◀ Although their territory was small, the Olmecs are thought to have influenced much of early Mesoamerican culture.

La Venta

Between around 800 and 400 BCE, La Venta was the most influential site in Central America. The site is dominated by a 100-foot (30 m) cone-shaped mound made from clay. Some experts believe it represents a volcano. To the north of the mound there is a plaza, as well as an enclosed area containing several tombs.

Looking out over the plaza are four enormous stone heads, weighing between fifteen and twenty tons and taller than the average person. Each head appears to be wearing a cap or helmet decorated with carvings, and their expressions add to their frightening appearance. With turned-down mouths, they look angry or unhappy. Carved stone ropes seem to be joining two of the heads, as if to represent close links between them. In another the ropes are tied to captives.

Food and Farming

Olmec people were skilled farmers. They grew crops on the naturally raised banks of the rivers where they lived. In summer, after these plots flooded, deposits of soil were left behind.

▶ *This eight-foot (2 m) high stone head may represent an Olmec ruler. The cap and downturned mouth were common features of Olmec carving.*

OLMECS

From 1500 BCE

First Olmec settlements are founded.

From 1150 BCE

San Lorenzo becomes a major trading center.

1000 BCE

La Venta is established as a cultural center.

By 700 BCE

San Lorenzo has started to decline.

From 500 BCE

Maya communities begin to develop.

By 350 BCE

La Venta is in rapid decline; some monuments are destroyed, possibly by the inhabitants.

Olmec people also built rafts and canoes so that they could travel over the ponds and rivers and catch fish and water birds to eat. On the drier land, just above river level, farmers grew maize. They could gather two harvests a year, one in the wet season and one in the dry season.

Art and Architecture

The Olmec rulers built big buildings and statues, partly to demonstrate their power to local people and partly to impress outsiders with their strength. Tall pyramids were built, as well as massive stone thrones. Material for these structures often came from quarries many miles away.

Many treasures from the Olmec period remain buried and hidden. In southern Veracruz archaeologists have found small jade statues, finely carved figures of clay, and blades made of obsidian.

FRANS BLOM AND OLIVER LA FARGE, TWO DANISH EXPLORERS WHO DISCOVERED OLMEC SITES IN 1925, DESCRIBE FINDING A MASSIVE CARVED STONE THRONE ON AN EIGHTY-TWO-FOOT (25 M) HIGH MOUND ON LA VENTA ISLAND.

[A guide showed us] a large block of stone. . . . We calculated the mass of the block to be at least 9 cubic metres. On its north side is an incised ornament along the upper rim of the table, and under this is a deep niche in which sits a human figure, legs crossed in Turkish fashion.

F. BLOM AND O. LA FARGE,
TRIBES AND TEMPLES

▶ *This head, known as Hahca, is a ritual symbol linked to Olmec ball games. On its cheek is a design of an endless knot of rope.*

THE MYSTERIOUS JAGUAR

The Olmecs probably respected the jaguar because it was the most ferocious and successful predator on land. Jaguars were stealthy and quick and difficult to avoid and to catch, and they could kill humans. (Other Olmec animal deities included the crocodile, a fierce water predator, and the eagle, a major predator in the air.) The Olmecs were the first people to give the jaguar godlike status. Early carvings show a mythical beast that is part jaguar, part serpent, part bird.

In Olmec art, jaguars symbolize the god of the rain and floods, on which people depended for crops and food. At an important Olmec trading site in Chalcatzingo in the state of Morelos, far to the west of the Olmec heartland, a cave has been hollowed out to represent the mouth of a jaguar, and inside sits the statue of a ruler. Water, symbolizing rain and the fertility it brings, pours from the jaguar's mouth.

Even as early as 1250 BCE, the Olmecs were making pottery and ceramics, as well as the massive carved stones. They also used kaolin (a type of fine white clay) to make small pottery figures and statues.

Other carvings were a fantastical mixture of animals and gods. Like much art of the ancient world, these elaborate and beautiful images were not merely decorative; they were almost certainly part of the ceremonies and rituals practiced by the Olmec people.

The Olmecs traded widely with neighboring peoples, and between 1100 and 800 BCE, their cultural influence spread northwest to the valley of Mexico and southeast to parts of Central America. The style of their religious carvings had a strong effect on later Central American cultures such as the Maya and the Aztecs.

SEE ALSO
- Maya

▶ An Olmec figure, carved from stone, of a mother sitting cross-legged, holding her baby.

Olympia

Olympia was one of the most important sites in ancient Greece. The settlement was founded during the Bronze Age, in about 1500 BCE, but it was the Olympic Games, which first took place in 776 BCE and then every four years afterward, that gave Olympia its lasting fame. Rhea, the Greek earth goddess, and Cronus, the god of the sky, were worshiped there. Their children, including Zeus, were the principal Greek gods who lived on Mount Olympus, in the northeast of Greece. Legend has it that Zeus's son Herakles (Hercules) marked out a six-hundred-foot-square (200 x 200 m) area and dedicated it to his "Olympian father," from which legend came the name Olympia.

A Sacred Sanctuary

In ancient times Olympia was a sacred area, or sanctuary, containing religious buildings of great importance. The most impressive was the Temple of Zeus, a huge limestone structure that was finished around 457 BCE. The interior was divided into three spaces: the entrance hall, the cella (the most sacred room), and a backroom where people left votive offerings to the gods. The cella contained the famous statue of Zeus, one of the Seven Wonders of the World. Created by the Athenian sculptor Phidias around 430 BCE, it was a forty-foot (12 m) tall image of Zeus, painted with gold hair and clothing and an ivory face and body. He was seated on a large wooden throne, also decorated in gold and ivory. In his right hand he held the figure of Nike, goddess of victory, and in his left there was an eagle-headed scepter. His feet were supported by two golden lions.

◀ In the mid-fourth century BCE, the architect Leonidas built a huge guest house in Olympia. Square in structure, it was surrounded by a colonnade of 138 columns, the bases of which can still be seen. It contained comfortable rooms for the honored guests of the games.

THE OLYMPIC GAMES

During the Olympic Games a truce (ekecheiria) was called, and the Greek states stopped all warfare for the festival. Until 724 BCE the only event was the stadion, a 220-yard (200 m) dash. In 708 BCE the pentathlon was introduced, a contest consisting of five events: running, a long jump, and discus, javelin, and quoit throwing. By far the most important contest was chariot racing, in which rich noblemen competed against each other in a specially built arena called a hippodrome.

After 472 BCE the festival was extended to five days. On the first day sacrifices were made to Zeus, while competitors took oaths that they would compete without cheating. On the second day the competitors' names were announced in the morning, and chariot racing and horse racing took place in the afternoon. On the third day teenagers competed in the boys' events, while the fourth saw all the main foot races (including one in full armor), and pankration (a mixture of boxing and wrestling). The fifth saw more sacrifices and an evening feast for the victors.

The Olympic Games remained popular in the ancient world until 393 CE, when the Roman emperor Theodosius I banned them. They were revived in 1896 in Athens.

The sanctuary also contained the Temple of Hera, a gymnasium, a square courtyard called a palaestra, baths, and a stadium for the games. The stadium was roughly 600 feet (180 m) long with earthen banks that accommodated up to 40,000 spectators. The start and finishing lines can still be seen.

◀ This black-figure amphora (storage jar) dates from the fifth century BCE. The height of the runners' knees and their outstretched arms suggest a foot race or sprint. Olympic scenes were popular and appear on much Greek pottery of this period.

SEE ALSO
- Greece, Classical
- Greek Mythology
- Sports and Entertainment
- Zeus

Palaces

A palace is a building or group of buildings in which a royal family lives; the name is also occasionally used for the grand residence of other important state officials. *Palace* derives from the Palatine Hill, in Rome, where in ancient times many Roman emperors built their magnificent residences.

First Palaces

The ancient Egyptians are thought to have been the first people to build palaces. Although the earliest palace seems to date from the reign of King Amenemhat III (1855–1808 BCE) at Bubastis in the Delta region of northern Egypt, most royal palaces date from the later New Kingdom, including those of Amenhotep III at Malkata, of his son Akhenaten at Amarna, of Merneptah at Memphis, and of Ramses III at Medinet Habu. The palaces of Amenhotep III and Ramses III are located at sites in western Thebes, a settlement in southern Egypt beside the Nile River.

These first palaces have several features that are repeated in other, later ones. They seem to have been surrounded by walls. Within these walls many small rooms were arranged around courtyards and gardens that were open to the sky. The large number of rooms suggests that each palace was a self-contained community. It provided accommodation for members of the royal family as well as for their servants, ministers, guards, visitors, and friends.

Symbols of Power

In time palaces became more than just places of residence. They were physical reminders, or symbols, of the ruler's power. For this reason each new ruler liked to build his or her own palace, with buildings as grand as possible. This custom reached a peak in ancient Rome. The palaces of the emperors of the first three centuries CE were more like small villages, spread over almost twenty-five acres (100,000 m²).

◀ *The Palatine Hill, Rome, where emperors liked to build their large and extravagant palaces.*

The sprawling remains of the palace of Amenhotep III (reigned 1390–1352 BCE) at Malkata, Thebes, reflect the great wealth enjoyed by Egypt during his reign.

To add to the grandeur of some palaces, they were built on a raised platform above the surrounding buildings, as were the Assyrian palace at Khorsabad and the Persian palaces at Persepolis.

Little Cities

In many cultures the royal palace was a center of government as well as a residence. In some societies it also had a religious significance. In ancient Egypt, for example, the pharaoh (king) was regarded as semidivine. Egyptian palaces often had a raised area from which the pharaoh could appear in public before his people. The palaces of eastern civilizations and of the Americas nearly all seem to have had governmental as well as religious and residential purposes.

The more functions a palace had, the more complicated it became. Perhaps the busiest of all was the Sacred Palace of Constantinople (Byzantium). It eventually covered some eighty-six acres (350,000 m²) and contained churches and schools as well as residences and meeting chambers.

THE MALKATA PALACE

The palace of King Amenhotep III of Egypt, built at Thebes on the Nile, is one of the oldest and best-preserved palaces in the world. Built largely of mud brick, as were all Egyptian houses, its huge numbers of buildings once covered a gigantic area. It consisted of several residences, a temple, a hall, houses, outbuildings, and even an artificial lake with its own harbor. The king and his principal wife, Tiy, had separate apartments. There was also accommodation for more than 350 of the king's minor wives and his many children and staff. Many of the walls were decorated with spectacular paintings of flowers and animals and inlaid with tiles and gilding.

SEE ALSO
- Amenhotep III • Egypt • Persepolis
- Rome, City of • Thebes

Parthians

The Parthians (Parni) were a nomadic people who lived around the southeastern shores of the Caspian Sea. Around 247 BCE a Parni chieftain named Arsaces led his people into present-day northern Iran, capturing the Persian city of Nisa from the Greek Seleucid Empire. This district was named Parthava, and its new Parni rulers were soon known by Greek and Roman writers as the Parthians.

The Arsacid Kingdom

Arsaces was the first of thirty-eight Parthian kings to rule between 247 BCE and the end of the Arsacid dynasty in 227 CE. The Arsacids quickly turned their small kingdom into a powerful empire. At its peak, the frontiers of Parthia stretched from Syria in the west to the great Indian trading city of Taxila in the east. The Parthians also controlled the Scythian kingdoms in central Asia between the Aral Sea and the Oxus River (modern-day Amu Darya). The wealth of the Parthian Empire was based on its control of the Silk Road, the trade route between Rome and China. During this period Parthia's power was rivaled only by that of Rome.

Government

The Parthian kings used the old city of Ecbatana (present-day Hamadan) in Media as their capital. Later kings spent the winter months at the fortress of Ctesiphon on the Tigris (present-day southern Iraq). A few noble families, who were closely related to the Arsacid kings and who owned vast estates, governed the kingdom. Land was parceled out in return for military service in wartime. The wealth of a Parthian noble was measured in the number of armed men that followed him into battle. Many of the nobles were superb horsemen, and they spent much of their time hunting and left the job of running their estates to Greek servants, who acted as secretaries.

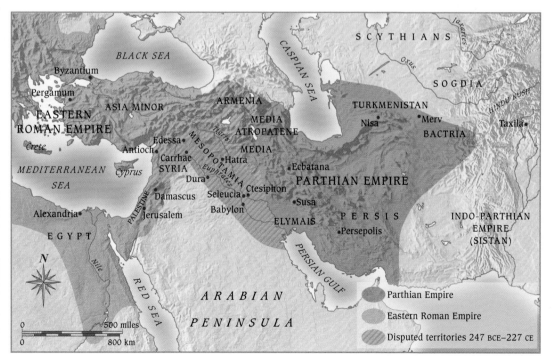

The Parthian Empire, about 100 CE. Between 247 BCE and 227 CE (the duration of the Arsacid dynasty) the Romans and the Parthians fought several battles for the territories that separated them.

The Parthians themselves left few written records. Most of what is known about them comes from Greek and Roman sources or from the careful study of Parthian coins.

The Cataphracts

Unlike the Greeks, Romans, and Persians, who fought mostly on foot, the Parthians preferred to fight on horseback. Their main troops were the cataphracts (from the Greek word *kataphraktos*, meaning "mail-clad"), cavalrymen from noble families who wore full suits of heavy chain mail. Special horses from Nesea were bred as heavy chargers and were also protected by armor. The cataphracts charged into battle armed with long lances, followed by units of horse archers. These horse archers were trained to continue firing arrows at high speed while pretending to flee in retreat before turning and facing the enemy again. Several Roman legions were lured into defeat by this tactic, which the Romans named "the Parthian shot."

War with Rome

Parthia and Rome spent many years at war with each other. The wealthy Roman businessman and politician Crassus hoped to win fame and popularity by defeating the Parthians. However, he was killed, and his army was destroyed, at the Battle of Carrhae in 53 BCE.

Mark Antony also failed to defeat the Parthians in 36 BCE. For short periods the Parthians even controlled the Roman provinces of Asia Minor, Syria, and Palestine in the eastern Mediterranean.

The Romans eventually forced the Parthians away from the Mediterranean coastline. Under Emperor Augustus the frontier between Parthia and Rome was established along the Euphrates River. However, the constant threat from Parthia forced the Romans to spend a great deal on defending their rich eastern provinces. The Romans tried to invade Parthia five more times, between 116 and 232 CE, but the expeditions all ended in failure, though the Romans managed to sack the Parthian city of Ctesiphon in 198.

The Fall of Parthia

After 200 CE many of the Parthian nobles defied their king and began to set up their own small kingdoms. In 224 CE a Persian prince named Ardashir Papakan successfully rebelled against the Parthian king Artabanus V. Within a few years almost all the lands of Parthia were ruled by Ardashir Papakan and his Sasanian successors.

▼ *The Parthian king Mithridates I, who ruled from 175 to 138 BCE, extended the frontiers of his kingdom to the Tigris and Euphrates valleys.*

PARTHIANS

c. 247 BCE

Arsaces leads Parni in successful revolt against governors of northern Iran.

178–138 BCE

Mithridates I secures Parthian control of Tigris and Euphrates valleys.

124–88 BCE

Mithridates II expands Parthian kingdom to its greatest extent.

96 BCE

Rome and Parthia clash for the first time, in a conflict over Syria.

92 BCE

Mithridates II signs a peace treaty with the Roman Republic.

53 BCE

Parthian cavalry units defeat Roman legions under Crassus at Carrhae (Harran).

40 BCE

Parthians capture Roman lands in the eastern Mediterranean.

36 BCE

Mark Antony invades Parthia but is forced to retreat.

114 CE

Parthians lose Armenia to Rome under Emperor Trajan.

198 CE

Romans sack Ctesiphon but are unable to hold the city.

224 CE

Persians under Ardashir revolt against Parthian rule.

228 CE

Last Parthian coins are issued by King Vologases VI.

MITHRIDATES II
REIGNED *124–88 BCE*

The greatest of the Arsacid kings of Parthia was Mithridates II (the Great). He secured Parthian control of Media and Persia and added Babylonia to his kingdom. He made alliances with the tribes of Sogdia and Bactria and extended Parthian power deep into central Asia and India. He claimed descent from the Achaemenid kings of Persia and adopted many Persian customs.

 *This rock carving, sculpted around 200 CE, shows a Parthian priest with nobles from the royal court and stands at Tang-e Sarvak in southwestern Iran.*

SEE ALSO

• Achaemenids • Alexander the Great
• Antony, Mark • Augustus • Sasanians
• Scythians

Pataliputra

Pataliputra is the ancient name of Patna, a city at the meeting point of two great Indian rivers, the Ganges and the Son. It was founded as a fort in the fifth century BCE by a king named Ajashatru. Later it grew into a city that became the capital of two ancient Indian empires, the Mauryan and the Gupta. Under the Mauryans in the third century BCE, it may well have been the world's largest city.

Mauryan Capital

Around 300 BCE a Greek named Megasthenes traveled to Pataliputra as the ambassador of his king, Seleucus. Megasthenes spent ten years living in the city and wrote a description of it in his book, *Indica*. Megasthenes was impressed by the comforts of life in Pataliputra. He described the houses of the rich, which had their own gardens, orchards, and ornamental ponds. The most impressive building in Pataliputra was the palace, which, like most of the buildings in the city, was built largely of wood. The palace had a great pillared hall, where the Mauryan emperors sat in state and received visitors.

According to Megasthenes, Pataliputra was approximately nine miles (15 km) long and one and a half miles (2.5 km) wide. It was protected by a huge timber palisade (wall of stakes), with 64 gateways, 570 towers, and many openings from which archers could shoot. The wall was surrounded in turn by a wide, deep moat. Since most of the buildings were made of wood, which has since rotted, little of the Mauryan capital has survived. Archaeologists have discovered traces of the palisade, as well as evidence of an elaborate drainage system. They have also found remains of the pillared hall of the palace, which is now underwater.

▶ *The modern city of Patna in northern India extends for twelve miles (19 km) along the southern bank of the Ganges River and stands on the site of ancient Pataliputra.*

Ashoka

Ashoka (c. 300–232 BCE), the third Mauryan emperor, converted to Buddhism and summoned monks from all over the empire to attend a meeting at Pataliputra. At this meeting, the Third Buddhist Council, Ashoka decided to send out missionaries to neighboring lands. Their greatest success was in converting the island of Sri Lanka, which has the longest continuous Buddhist history of any country.

Later History

After the breakup of the Mauryan Empire, Pataliputra remained the capital of the small kingdom of Magadha. According to some historians, in 185 BCE the city was briefly captured by an invading army of Greeks, led by Menander, king of Bactria (in present-day northern Afghanistan).

Pataliputra was revived under Chandra Gupta I, who made it the capital city of the Gupta Empire around 320 CE. It began to decline again in the late fourth century, when the fourth emperor, Chandra Gupta II, moved his capital to Ujjain in central India. By the seventh century the city had been abandoned. It remained deserted until it was refounded, as Patna, in 1541.

▶ *Like Fa-Hsien, many Chinese Buddhist monks went on pilgrimages to India, the birthplace of their religion. The monk in this painting carries holy scriptures on his back and a fly whisk to drive away demons on his long and dangerous journey.*

SEE ALSO

- Ashoka
- Gupta Empire
- Mauryan Empire

FA-HSIEN, A CHINESE BUDDHIST PILGRIM, VISITED PATALIPUTRA IN ABOUT 400 CE. AMAZED BY THE BEAUTY OF THE ANCIENT MAURYAN PALACE, HE COULD NOT BELIEVE IT HAD BEEN BUILT BY HUMAN BEINGS:

Ashoka's royal palace and halls in the midst of the city, which stand now as of old, were all made by spirits which he employed, and which heaped up stones, raised walls and gates, and made the elegant carving and inlaid sculpture work—all in a way no human hand of this world could have accomplished.

FA-HSIEN, A RECORD OF THE BUDDHISTIC KINGDOMS

Paul of Tarsus

Paul of Tarsus was born in about 10 CE and died in about 67. He was educated in the manner of both a Jewish scholar and a Greek philosopher and man of letters. He was also a Roman citizen. The lives of Paul and Jesus overlapped, but they never met. Paul became a Christian shortly after Jesus' death, in the early 30s. Paul's life is described in the New Testament, in the Acts of the Apostles.

On his mission to convert the Gentiles to Christianity, Paul made three major journeys across the eastern Roman Empire and traveled farther than any emperor or general of his day.

Paul's Early Life
Paul was born to a Jewish family in Tarsus, in present-day Turkey. As a young man, he became a rabbi and was in Jerusalem around the time of Jesus' crucifixion. The first Christians were saying that Jesus was the Son of God. The Jewish authorities thought these Christians were blasphemers, and Paul agreed. In 35 he looked on while Stephen, a Christian accused of blasphemy, was stoned to death. Stephen is honored as the first Christian martyr.

Paul's Conversion
One day Paul was traveling to Damascus to arrest some Christians. Suddenly a blinding light shone out of the sky, and he saw a vision of Jesus, who asked why Paul was persecuting him. When Paul reached Damascus, he started preaching the message of Jesus Christ. The Jewish authorities tried to arrest him, but his Christian friends smuggled him out of the city by lowering him over the walls in a basket.

Jews, Converts, and Gentiles
Jews lived according to the Torah, the Jewish Law. They obeyed strict rules, particularly concerning what they ate. Jewish law also required all boys to be circumcised eight days after birth. Almost all the first Christians were Jewish converts, who were

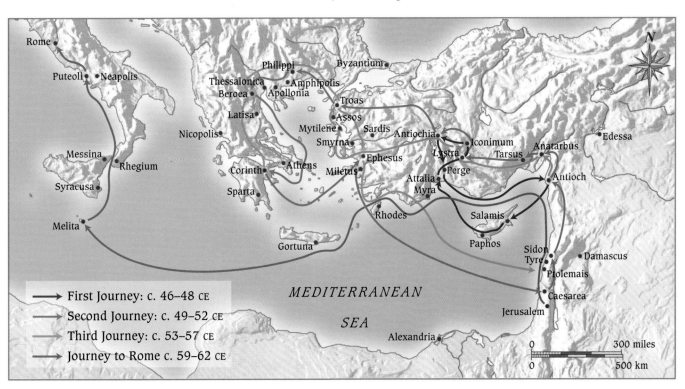

First Journey: c. 46–48 CE
Second Journey: c. 49–52 CE
Third Journey: c. 53–57 CE
Journey to Rome c. 59–62 CE

known as Nazarenes. When Paul began inviting Gentiles (non-Jews) to become Christians, the Nazarenes were shocked, as Jews were forbidden to share a meal with Gentiles. The question arose whether converts to Christianity must first embrace Jewish law (including the circumcision requirement).

The leaders of the early Christian church (the Apostles Peter, James, and John) held a conference in Jerusalem and requested that Paul exclude Gentiles from his churches. Paul argued that the success of his churches showed that it was right to include Gentiles. He persuaded Peter and the others that Gentiles did not have to be circumcised to become Christians.

The End of Paul's Life

Throughout his life Paul's work angered the Jews. Having set up churches in cities all over the Roman Empire, in about 60 CE he went to Jerusalem, where he was arrested. As a Roman citizen he was taken to Rome to be tried under Roman law, although it seems that he was never tried but was simply kept in prison. In 64 CE the emperor Nero, blaming the Christians for a huge fire that destroyed much of Rome, had many Christians killed. It is believed that Paul died in the course of this persecution.

▶ *Paul is being led to martyrdom in this fourth-century relief from the tomb of the Roman prefect Junius Bassus.*

SEE ALSO
• Christianity • Jesus of Nazareth

PAUL'S EPISTLES

After his conversion Paul's mission became the conversion of people to Christianity. He established Christian churches all over the Roman Empire. Paul's letters, or epistles, to his churches became part of the New Testament, the specifically Christian part of the Bible. In these letters he explains his doctrine of "all the same in Christ," meaning that all, whatever their former creed, are equal in the Christian Church.

Pericles

Pericles was born into a wealthy, aristocratic Athenian family about 495 BCE and died in 429. He received an excellent education, especially from the philosopher Anaxagoras. Though the first part of his adult life was spent as a soldier, Pericles was a man of wide-ranging interests: in 472, aged about twenty-three, he paid for a set of plays to be performed at the city's drama festival. A few years later he led a lawsuit against Cimon, a well-known Athenian who was accused of corruption.

▼ With his helmet pushed back on his head, Pericles is both war leader and politician in this fifth-century-CE marble bust, a Roman copy of a Greek original.

Defender of Democracy

At this time Athens was developing a system of government known as democracy, in which every citizen was entitled to vote on each proposed law and to elect the most important officials.

Soon Pericles joined other Athenian politicians who were seeking to limit the power of an ancient unelected government committee called the Areopagus. This committee had traditionally overseen the appointment of state officials and prosecuted them for misconduct. As a result of the reforms that Pericles helped bring about, the power of the Areopagus was greatly reduced.

Later Pericles also recommended that those who served on juries in Athens's many court cases should be paid for doing so, because he wanted even the poorest Athenians to be able to serve their city.

At this time the Athenians received tribute money from other Greek states under their protection. Pericles persuaded his fellow citizens to use part of this wealth to pay for the reconstruction of the buildings on the Acropolis, the holy hill at the center of Athens, which had been destroyed by the Persians. Under his guidance arose temples and other structures—such as the Parthenon—that have been the admiration of the world ever since.

◀ Sculptors, philosophers, and poets form a crowd around Pericles in this nineteeth-century print. The newly completed buildings of the Acropolis can be seen in the background.

The End of Pericles' Life

From 443 BCE until his death in 429 BCE, Pericles was reelected by the people almost every year as one of their military and political leaders. He died of the plague during the long siege of Athens by the Spartans.

Pericles was a man of wide interests and outstanding abilities who worked tirelessly for his city and state. He was a remarkably persuasive speaker, as he had to be, for Athens's system of democracy required him to justify his proposals and actions not merely before a committee, senate, or parliament but to meetings of three thousand or more citizens, meetings that were held on a monthly basis.

SEE ALSO

• Acropolis • Athens

THE HISTORIAN THUCYDIDES ATTRIBUTED THE FOLLOWING DESCRIPTION OF HOW ATHENS WAS RULED TO PERICLES:

. . . we are called a democracy, for the government is in the hands of the many not the few . . . when a citizen is in any way distinguished, he is promoted to the public service, not as a matter of privilege, but as a reward of merit. Neither is poverty an obstacle, for a man may benefit his country whatever the obscurity of his position. . . .

And we have not forgotten to provide for our weary spirits relaxation from toil; we have regular games and sacrifices throughout the year; our homes are beautiful and elegant; and the delight we daily feel in all these things helps to banish sorrow.

THUCYDIDES, *HISTORY OF THE PELOPONNESIAN WAR*, 2:34–36

Persepolis

Persepolis is the better-known Greek name for Parsa, a site composed of a set of palaces built to show the power and wealth of the Persian kings. The ruins of Parsa lie in the present-day Iranian province of Fars, thirty-five miles (56 km) northeast of the city of Shiraz and twenty-seven miles (43 km) from the tomb of Cyrus the Great at Pasargadae.

A Royal Showcase

The Achaemenid kings used the old, established cities of Susa and Babylon as their centers of government and religion. Their summer residence was at Ecbatana (modern-day Hamadan in western Iran). Although Persepolis was the main seat of government of the Persian Empire, it was not the only royal city. It was, however, a monument to the greatness of the Achaemenid dynasty.

The entire complex of Persepolis sits high on a raised terrace of cut stone that looks out across the dry plains of central Persia. The walls still carry giant relief sculptures of the Persian royal family. Other reliefs show soldiers in the Persian army, as well as subjects from the twenty-eight nations that were once ruled by the Achaemenids.

Building at Persepolis began around 520 BCE in the reign of Darius I (522–486). However, his son Xerxes (486–465 BCE) and grandson Artaxerxes I (465–425 BCE) built most of what still survives at the site.

Royal Ceremony

Some scholars think that Persepolis was used only a few days each year for the ceremony of Nowruz, or New Year's Day. Nowruz marked the beginning of spring and was a great day of feasting in honor of

▶ This vivid carving of a lion attacking a bull, one of many that still adorn the ruins of Persepolis, decorates the eastern staircase that leads to the Apadana, the royal audience hall.

the Persian god Ahura Mazda. Sitting in his throne hall, the king received the leading nobles and governors from every province of the empire as well as ambassadors from other kingdoms. The gifts they brought as tribute were then carefully stored in the treasury of the royal palace.

Visitors passed along monumental stairways and corridors and through the Gate of all Nations. The king's subjects massed in the Apadana, the great audience hall. Once the rituals of Nowruz were complete, the king and his courtiers moved back to Susa, leaving Persepolis in the hands of a few trusted guards.

Ruin and Decay

Alexander the Great captured Persepolis in 330 BCE. His army set fire to the site and destroyed it so thoroughly that it was never rebuilt. The ruins remained largely undisturbed until the Dutch traveler Cornelis de Bruijn visited and drew them in 1705 CE.

In the twentieth century parts of this impressive site were reconstructed and restored to their former glory.

ARTAXERXES I

REIGNED 465–425 BCE

Artaxerxes became king of Persia through murder and intrigue. His father, Xerxes, was mysteriously assassinated at the height of his powers in 465 BCE. Artaxerxes immediately accused his older brother of the crime, had him executed, and took his place on the throne.

To try to convince everyone that he was the rightful ruler, he took the name Artaxerxes, which means "having just rule." He also spent much of his time and money completing the palaces at Persepolis, in order to emphasize the links between himself and the other great Achaemenid kings.

▲ *Visitors to Persepolis were surrounded by images of subjects paying homage to the Persian king. Babylonian, Lydian, and Sogdian delegates are shown presenting lavish gifts.*

SEE ALSO

• Achaemenids
• Ahura Mazda
• Alexander the Great
• Cyrus the Great
• Darius I
• Palaces
• Xerxes

Petra

The city of Petra lies hidden among the rocks of southwestern Jordan. Rediscovered by the Swiss traveler Johann Burckhardt in 1812, Petra can be reached only through a narrow fissure (gap) in the towering three-hundred-foot (100 m) rock face known as the Siq. The path twists and turns until it suddenly opens out into a wide, sheltered basin containing a city with houses, staircases, theaters, and tombs carved out of rose-colored sandstone.

The Creators of the Hidden City

The Nabataeans, once nomadic goat herders, used the valley in the rock as a refuge in a hostile desert environment. Gradually they became highly successful traders, taking huge caravans of men and camels across the deserts. By the fourth century BCE, in control of the important route from Petra to Gaza on the Mediterranean coast, they exchanged goods with trading partners in southern Arabia and exported copper and bitumen (a tarlike substance extracted from rock) to Egypt. There was also a huge market for expensive commodities such as incense, myrrh, and spices in Greece and Italy to the north.

The Nabataeans extended their trading activities until, by the early second century BCE, they commanded the routes across the Sinai and Nefud Deserts and southern Syria and into Arabia as far as Hegra to the south and Duma to the east. The wealth they accumulated enabled them to build the city of Petra.

From Refuge to City

The most important requirement for a city in a dry, rocky environment was an ade-

To the east of the city of Petra is a complex of six tombs cut into the cliffs. Some of these probably contained the remains of the Nabataean kings. On the right, the tall Classical Urn Tomb can be seen, and on the far left, the Corinthian Tomb.

MONUMENTS TO THE DEAD

The most spectacular remains still visible in Petra are the royal mausoleums (funerary monuments), cut out of the pink sandstone cliffs. The largest is the Deir, 148 feet (45 m) wide and 138 feet (42 m) tall. This mausoleum dates from the first century CE. That many of the mausoleums are built in the classical Greek style, with smooth facades, columns, and pediments, is evidence of the great influence of Greece on the traders of Petra.

◀ A stepped processional way leads to a courtyard in front of the Deir. The huge facade contains a doorway 26 feet (8 m) tall leading into a chamber hewn out of the rock.

quate water supply. The water was provided by a huge system of cisterns filled by springs, wadis (streams that fill only in the rainy season), and rainwater. The rainwater ran off the hard rock into specially cut channels and gutters, which filled the closed cisterns. A large network of clay pipes brought the water from the cisterns safely into the center of the city by way of a *nymphaeum* (public fountain).

The main street of the city followed the path of the Musa riverbed from east to west. On either side were temples, markets, shops, shrines, and a royal palace. Behind this city center, archaeologists have found large stone townhouses with pillared courtyards and reception rooms. Many simpler dwellings were carved into the surrounding cliffs. At its peak, Petra may have had between 10,000 and 20,000 inhabitants.

Decline

Petra was officially taken into the Roman Empire in 106 CE, under Emperor Trajan. It ceased to be an important caravan center and was abandoned after it was seriously damaged by an earthquake in 551 CE. It was forgotten for nearly 1300 years.

SEE ALSO
- Egypt
- Greece, Classical
- Roman Republic and Empire
- Trade

Philip II of Macedon

When Philip II came to the throne in 359 BCE he saved his country from rebellion and invasion and soon built an army so formidable that he was able to conquer the whole of Greece. Yet Philip's son achieved so much more that Philip's own achievements are often forgotten. That son was Alexander the Great.

Youth

Born in 382 BCE, Philip was the son of King Amyntas II of Macedonia. Throughout his early life his father and brothers were engaged in battles against both internal and external enemies. Philip was caught up in these wars, and for about two years, as a young teenager, he was held hostage in Thebes. His observations of the excellent military training of the Theban army may have influenced the changes he later made to his own.

A Soldier King

When Philip first became king, he faced immense problems: warring chiefs, enemies on the borders, territory lost. However, using great skill in warfare and diplomacy, he succeeded in meeting these challenges. He gave way when he had to, made alliances where he could, and created a magnificent army to defend his own state and conquer others.

Philip made his army professional. He paid his soldiers well, trained them to a high standard, and developed new military techniques. He made the traditional infantry formation, the phalanx (a block of foot soldiers that move forward as one against the enemy), larger and more flexible. He armed his infantry with the *sarissa*, a pike eighteen feet (4 m) long, so that the enemy could be engaged at a distance. Furthermore, the infantry was defended at its weakest points by the cavalry (soldiers who fight on horseback). For this cavalry force he recruited the sons of nobles and educated and trained them at his court. This treatment encouraged loyalty and friendship and enabled Philip to mold these young men exactly as he wanted.

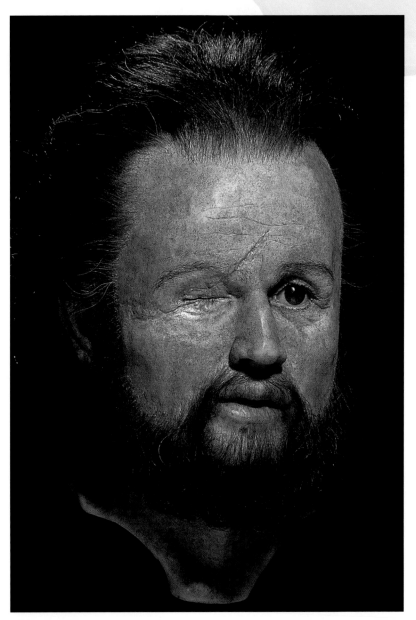

▼ The bones of Philip II's skull were used as a guide to construct this model of his head.

Soon Philip was dominating states deep within Greece. Then, at the Battle of Chaeronea in 338 BCE, he defeated a combined Athenian and Theban army and gained control over all the Greek states.

Philip's Legacy

Philip was murdered in 336 BCE by Pausanias, a young Macedonian who had a private quarrel with the king. Philip's achievements laid the foundations for Alexander's greatness. Philip created peace and stability in Macedonia. He also provided his son with a strong army that could be used to bring the whole of Greece under his authority.

▼ *None of Philip II's coins showed his own head; this example has an image of a youthful god, probably Apollo.*

OLYMPIAS *c. 375–316 BCE*

Olympias, the daughter of the king of Epirus, near modern Albania, married Philip in 357 BCE. She claimed to be descended from Achilles and worshiped Dionysus, the god of wine. Soon after the birth of their son, Alexander, she tried to convince Philip that the true father of the child was the Greek-Egyptian god Zeus-Ammon. Such a belief probably worried Philip but may also have encouraged Alexander to believe that he was divine.

Philip had several other wives apart from Olympias. In 336 BCE he decided to marry a girl named Cleopatra, the daughter of a Macedonian nobleman. There was talk that any future son of Cleopatra's might be preferred to Alexander as the next king. Olympias went back to her native Epirus after a quarrel with Philip. Soon afterward the king was murdered, and Olympias returned to see Alexander crowned king of Macedon.

SEE ALSO

• Alexander the Great
• Greece, Classical
• Macedonians

Phoenicians

Phoenicia was situated largely in present-day Lebanon but also included parts of modern Syria and Israel. The Phoenicians were great seamen and traders who colonized the Mediterranean region during the first millennium BCE. Their civilization flourished from around 3000 BCE until it was absorbed into the Roman Empire in 64 BCE. The name Phoenicians means "the purple people" and was given to them by the Greeks because of the purple dye the Phoenicians extracted from the murex shellfish. The Phoenicians' most lasting achievement was the development of the alphabet from which the Greek, Latin, Hebrew, and Arabic alphabets are derived. The chief Phoenician towns were Tyre, Byblos, Sidon, and Berot (modern Beirut).

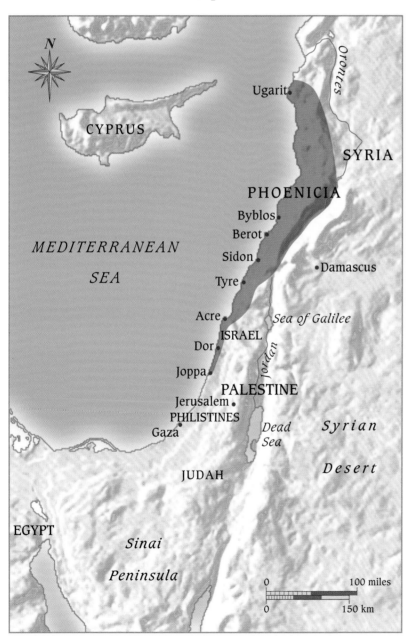

▼ *Phoenicia at the height of its powers in 1100 BCE.*

The Rise and Fall of Phoenicia

Although they had writing, the Phoenicians left no historical account of themselves. Ancient historians, such as Herodotus, believed that the Phoenicians originally came from the Persian Gulf. Their first settlement was probably Byblos, whose founding dates to around the third millennium BCE. By the second millennium BCE they had established settlements along the coast of the Levant.

The Phoenicians began trading with nearby Egypt in the second millennium. During this period they were governed or at least dominated by the pharaohs of Egypt. Phoenicia was important to the Egyptian kingdom because of its abundant supplies of timber, grain, fruit, and cattle. For the next five hundred years Egyptian authority came and went in Phoenicia, as at various times other invaders attacked and took over the Phoenician settlements or demanded tribute from them. Beginning in the ninth century BCE, the remaining Egyptian influence in the area first waned and then died away altogether.

PHOENICIANS

2613–2494 BCE

Phoenicians establish commercial and religious connections with Egypt.

c. 2000 BCE

Phoenicians found a series of settlements along the coast of the Levant—Joppa, Dor, Acre, and Ugarit.

c. 1600 BCE

Egypt trades with and controls Phoenicia.

c. 1400 BCE

Egypt's hold over Phoenicia relaxes.

1100 BCE

Phoenicians dominate the eastern Mediterranean.

c. 1000 BCE

Utica, the oldest Phoenician colony, is established in modern-day Tunisia.

c. 900 BCE

Assyria threatens Phoenicia's independence.

573 BCE

Tyre falls to the Babylonians.

538 BCE

Phoenicia comes under Persian rule.

332 BCE

Tyre is besieged by Alexander the Great.

206 BCE

Carthage is defeated by Rome.

146 BCE

Carthage is destroyed.

64 BCE

Phoenicia is incorporated into the Roman Empire.

c. 500 CE

Phoenician language dies out.

THE PHOENICIANS AS SEAFARERS

For the Phoenicians, with several sophisticated city-states along the coast of present-day Lebanon, the sea provided a vital means of transport. They built wooden boats, chiefly trading ships with a single mast and oars to steer. They also built warships with two banks of oars for speed and control in battle.

Besides developing ships capable of traveling thousands of miles, the Phoenicians discovered the use of the North Star, located directly above the North Pole, as an essential aid to navigation.

The Phoenicians possibly sailed around Africa some time in the sixth century BCE, probably traveled as far as the Azores and Britain, and built harbors in Sidon and Tyre. Toward the end of their colonizing period, they built a series of lighthouses in their settlements to mark the coastline for their ships. These structures were probably just wooden bonfires lit at night but may have been towers built specially for the purpose. The Phoenicians' reputation as pirates may have come about because their history was written by their rivals for control of the sea.

▲ This relief carving of a Phoenician merchant ship shows the single sail and steering oars.

During the ninth century BCE Phoenician power came to the fore. The cities of Phoenicia—Tyre, Byblos, Berot, and Sidon—had their own kings and paid tribute to no one. Tyre began to establish its own colonies around the Mediterranean, and other colonies were established at Carthage in North Africa and in Anatolia (present-day eastern Turkey) and Cyprus.

In the late ninth century BCE the Phoenicians were threatened by the Assyrian kingdom and regularly had to pay tribute to them. It was this need to find gold and other precious metals that drove the Phoenicians to sail farther and farther afield in search of good places to trade and establish new colonies. For two centuries waves of Assyrian invaders marched across Phoenicia, gaining control of the major cities for short periods.

In 538 BCE Phoenicia came under the dominance of the Persians. By this time Sidon had become the most powerful of the Phoenician cities, and its ships and sailors served in the navy of the Persian king Xerxes in the invasion of Greece. In the next century there were rebellions against the Persians in Phoenician cities, but they failed.

Two Empires

Tyre fell to Alexander the Great in 332 BCE, and Phoenicia then became a part of the Macedonian Empire. In 64 BCE the next great empire, the Romans, took charge of the area. Phoenicia became part of a larger Roman province, Syria, but the great cities of Tyre and Sidon remained independent. Carthage created its own empire, which competed with Rome for control of the western Mediterranean.

The ancient city of Berot, renamed Berytus in Latin, grew in importance when the emperor Augustus made it a colony of Rome. Later, in the first century CE, Sidon and Tyre also became Roman colonies. Phoenicia remained part of the Roman Empire until its fall.

Trade and Crafts

As traders the Phoenicians brought sophisticated goods to their cities: silk, perfumes, and spices from the Orient and ebony, ivory, amber, precious stones, metals, ostrich eggs, and horses from North Africa. Phoenician craftsmen made limestone carvings as well as gold jewelry copied from Egyptian and Oriental sources featuring animal motifs. They knew how to make blown glass by the first century BCE. They also made linen cloth, which they dyed purple and embroidered, and were famed for their carved ivory objects and wooden furniture.

▼ The ruins of ancient Byblos in present-day Lebanon. Byblos was a major Phoenician trading port from which cedar and papyrus were exported.

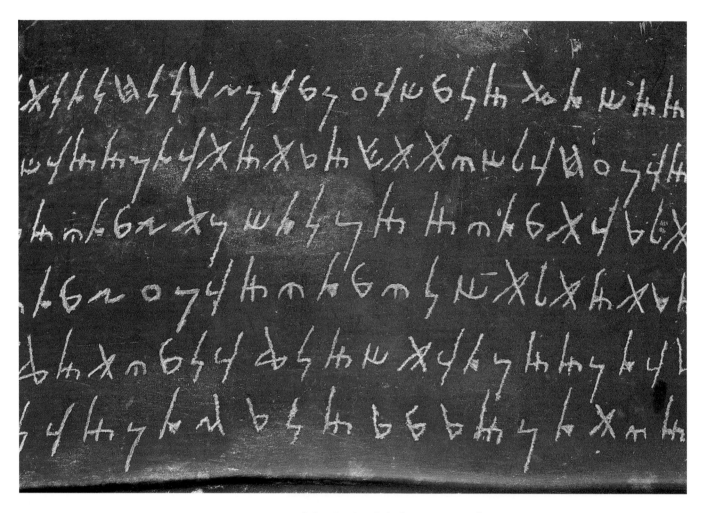

Language

The Phoenicians spoke a Semitic language very similar to Hebrew. At first it was written using cuneiform (a form of writing that came from Mesopotamia) and later a twenty-two-letter alphabet, the forerunner of the Latin alphabet now used in Europe. The Phoenicians wrote from right to left, and their written words had no symbols for vowel sounds. The earliest example of Phoenician writing was found at Byblos and dates back to 1100 BCE.

▲ *This Phoenician sarcophagus inscription avows that Eshmunazar and his mother, Amashtarte, were servants of the goddess Astarte and built temples dedicated to her and to other Phoenician gods.*

PHOENICIAN RELIGION

The Phoenicians worshiped a family of gods led by the father of the gods, El. Their most worshiped god was Astarte (known in Carthage as Tanit), a fertility goddess. Another of their gods was Melqart (known in Carthage as Baal Hammon), god of the sun and of death and also the husband of the goddess Astarte. There was a temple to Melqart at Tyre, where spring and autumn festivals were dedicated to him.

SEE ALSO

- Alexander the Great • Carthage
- Egypt
- Roman Republic and Empire
- Ships and Boats
- Trade • Tyre
- Xerxes

Plato

Little is known for certain about Plato's life. Born in 427 BCE, he was a Greek poet who turned to philosophy as a follower of Socrates. When Socrates was executed by the democrats in 399 because of his aristocratic contacts, Plato left Athens and traveled widely before returning to Greece. Around 386 Plato founded a school of philosophy, the Academy, just outside Athens. He taught there until his death, in about 347 BCE. Aristotle was a student at this "first university."

▼ This sculpture of Plato's head, carved in the first century CE, is a Roman copy of a Greek original.

Plato's Writings

Plato wrote his books of philosophy from about 396 BCE until his death. One of them, the *Apology*, is an imagined account of Socrates' trial. Another, titled the *Crito* after Plato's friend Criton, describes Socrates in prison, refusing—for moral reasons—to try to escape. The *Phaedo* records Socrates arguing that the soul is immortal and poignantly describes the moment when he was condemned to take poison.

Philosophical Questions

Plato used the fictional dialogue form in order to portray people thinking and arguing aloud in vigorous discussions full of life and humor. He showed Socrates, in the company of his students, wrestling with such questions as "Can one teach people to live well?" "How can one know anything?" "What is true justice?" "What is the best kind of government?" and "What is the best kind of education?"

In his writings Plato returns again and again to one question, "What is reality?" He came to believe that real things exist only in an ideal spiritual world. For example, he argues that if all horses or all desks are different from each other, the only real thing about them must be some characteristic that they all share—"horseness" or "deskness." This essential characteristic is an "idea" that cannot be seen or touched. Reality therefore has to be "ideal," a matter of ideas, or as Plato named them, forms.

An Imaginary State

In the *Republic*, his best-known book, Plato imagined a perfectly run state. Such a state would be arranged into three classes, or levels. The ruling class would be a group of philosophers, whom Plato named the perfect guardians. Their philosophical education would enable them to know what was morally good for everyone, and so they would be given the authority to create the laws of the state. They would also share all their property, wives, and children. A second class, named the auxiliary guardians, would assist the perfect guardians and defend the state. Remaining would be a third class, workers and merchants, who would farm the land, produce goods, and engage in trade.

IN THE *PHAEDO* THE CONDEMNED SOCRATES DISCUSSES THE SOUL'S IMMORTALITY BEFORE DRINKING POISON IN FRONT OF HIS GRIEF-STRICKEN FRIENDS:

Apollodorus, who had been weeping quietly all this time, broke out into loud sobs, and everyone present did the same—except Socrates himself. He simply said, "What a scene! Amazing! . . . Please calm down and put up with all this quietly." When we heard him, we were ashamed and tried to hold back our tears. He walked about a little, then . . . lay down on his back, as the man had told him to.

PLATO, *PHAEDO*

◀ This first-century-BCE Roman mosaic from Pompeii shows Plato with his pupils.

SEE ALSO

- Aristotle • Athens
- Education
- Greece, Classical
- Greek Philosophy
- Pythagoras
- Socrates

Polynesian Culture

Situated east of Melanesia and Micronesia, Polynesia is a large, triangular-shaped area in the Pacific Ocean that extends north of Hawaii, south of New Zealand, and eastward past Easter Island. The ancient Polynesians originated more than 2,500 years ago and during more than a millennium and a half traveled through the region and settled on its many islands.

A Great Expansion

Descended from the Lapita peoples, the Polynesians reached the islands of western Polynesia, particularly Samoa and Tonga, between 2,500 and 3,000 years ago. From around 200 BCE onward, there was a great expansion. Traveling in large wooden canoes, the Polynesians reached Tahiti and other islands in the Society Islands group between 500 and 600 CE, Easter Island and Hawaii by 800, and New Zealand between 1100 and 1300.

Polynesian Food and Homes

The Polynesians were farmers, gatherers, and fishermen. They went out fishing in canoes and also fished in stone traps and ponds built in lagoons. They ate the fruits of plants found on their islands, which included coconut palms, wild fruit trees, and berry plants, but most of their food came from crops such as taro, breadfruit, and bananas. Coconuts provided both food and liquid. Furthermore, the hairy husks were a source of fiber with which to make cord, the tree trunks provided frames for building homes, and the leaves made a covering for the roofs and walls.

Polynesian Society

The ancient Polynesians developed societies governed by strict rules and led by chiefs

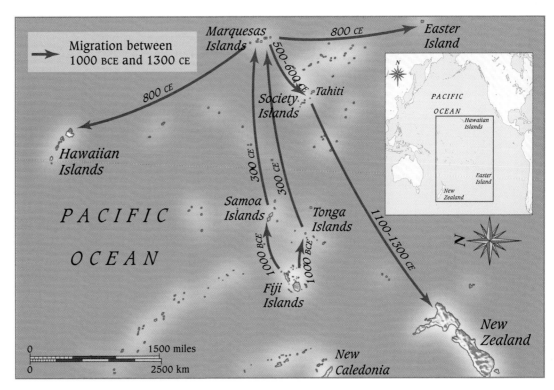

▶ Polynesian migration and settlements, 1000 BCE–1300 CE.

3500   3000   2500   2000   1500   1000   500   1   500

who were feared and obeyed. The notions of mana (spiritual power) and *tapu* (rules designed to stop damage from occurring to mana) guided the lives of the people. Everybody had some mana, but chiefs had the most. On some islands, if an ordinary person touched the chief's shadow, the only way to correct the damage done to the chief's mana was to kill that person. Other common *tapus* were not to eat certain foods or to visit certain places. Animals and everyday things also had mana, and to step over a tool lying on the ground was believed to make it useless.

POLYNESIANS

c. 1000–500 BCE

Rise of Polynesian civilization.

500–600 CE

Polynesians reach Tahiti and the Marquesas Islands.

800 CE

First wave of Polynesians reach Hawaii and Easter Island.

1100–1600 CE

Moai statues built on Easter Island.

The only beings that possessed greater mana than the chief were the spirit beings and the gods that the Polynesians believed in. The Polynesians had many gods; they were worshiped at simple temples with rituals that involved chants, feasting, and sometimes sacrifices of animals or even human beings.

POLYNESIAN NAVIGATION

The Polynesians navigated their way through the Pacific using their knowledge of the natural world, built up over centuries, to guide them on their journeys. Like their ancestors, the Lapita peoples, they recognized and understood different winds and wave conditions and also knew how to follow seabirds who returned to land after feeding late in the day. The Polynesians had names for over 200 stars and knew when these stars rose and set and how they moved across the night sky according to the seasons. Archaeologists believe that using the stars as a guide to movement was vital to the Polynesians' success as navigators.

▼ This carved wooden model of an ancient Polynesian war canoe was made in New Zealand in the nineteenth century and features a highly decorated prow (the front part of the boat).

Magic and Cannibalism

Many Polynesian adults performed magic rituals believed to bring success in war, fishing, and the planting and growing of crops. There were also rituals designed to bring misfortune or illness to others. Some Polynesians practiced cannibalism, though on some islands, such as Tahiti, cannibalism was rare. It was believed that those who ate the flesh of an enemy would inherit his or her mana. Eating the body of a hated rival was considered the ultimate revenge.

EASTER ISLAND

▼ These distinctive Moai statues are found on the slopes of the Rano Raraku crater in Easter Island. They were sculpted from the rock found inside the crater.

A sixty-four-square-mile (166 km²) triangle of volcanic rock in the South Pacific, Easter Island lies more than two thousand miles (3,200 km) away from both Tahiti and the coast of Chile and is the most remote inhabited place on earth. Yet by around 800 CE Polynesians had settled here, on the island they named Te Pito O Te Henua ("navel of the world"). A distinct culture developed on Easter Island, with intricate stone carvings, a type of hieroglyphic writing called rongo-rongo, and the building of ahus, ceremonial stone burial platforms, mainly around the coast. From 1100 CE onward, almost nine hundred giant stone statues, called moai, were carved out of the rock at Rano Raraku, a sunken volcano crater. Each of the statues stands around thirteen feet (3.9 m) in height and weighs about 14 tons (14.2 tonnes). Most of the statues feature a distinctive, long-nosed, sunken-eyed face. As many as 288 of these figures were transported across the rocky island to be erected on ahus, an amazing feat considering their size and weight. There are several theories about how and why the islanders carved and moved so many of these beautiful and haunting statues.

SEE ALSO
- Lapita Culture
- Melanesian Culture
- Micronesian Culture
- Transportation

Pompeii

Pompeii was a small Roman town in the south of Italy. The thriving center of its region, in 79 CE Pompeii was destroyed by the eruption of Vesuvius, a nearby volcano. The ruins of Pompeii have given archaeologists a unique insight into Roman life.

Origins of Pompeii

Pompeii's origins probably date from the 700s BCE. The site chosen for the first settlement was the flat top of a plateau, near the sea. For hundreds of years, the settlement was little more than a Grecian-influenced coastal village, a convenient place for sailors to stop. During the 300s BCE the Samnites took control of the area; they extensively rebuilt Pompeii and added many streets and buildings. By 150 BCE Pompeii had become the region's main port, with a harbor that was also used by neighboring towns. Agriculture was important to Pompeii's economy, and wine was one of its main exports. The town prospered and became a popular place for Romans to enjoy themselves. Among the public buildings erected were a forum, a theater, temples, baths, and an amphitheater. About 20,000 people lived there.

Destruction of Pompeii

In 62 CE an earthquake shook Pompeii. No one knew that this earthquake was a sign that Vesuvius, five miles (8 km) to the north, was stirring. At about noon on August 24, 79 CE, the volcano erupted. Day turned to night as pumice (a lightweight rock) and ash rained down, the dust covering Pompeii in a gray layer eight feet (2.5 m) deep. Roofs collapsed and fires started. Most of the population had time to escape, but some people chose to remain, walking about on top of the pumice layer. Only the tops of tall buildings were visible.

◀ Years of careful excavation have removed the volcanic debris from much of the town of Pompeii and revealed the ruins of streets, shops, houses, temples, and baths.

Plaster casts of the bodies of two victims of the eruption. Although most people fled to safety, some stayed behind—and paid with their lives.

The end came at about 7:30 the following morning, when the first of three flows of volcanic debris overwhelmed Pompeii. The two thousand people still in the town suffocated or were burned to death. Pompeii vanished, buried beneath about 30 feet (10 m) of debris. The town no longer existed, and people eventually forgot it was there.

Pompeii Uncovered

In 1748 Pompeii was rediscovered. The first treasure hunters searched for art objects and wall paintings, which were removed and sent to museums. Later excavators, working to uncover the plan of the town, revealed its streets and buildings. When Giuseppe Fiorelli (1823–1896) excavated Pompeii in the 1860s and 1870s, he realized that hollows in the pumice were where people's bodies had once been. By pumping plaster of paris into the spaces he made casts of Pompeiians who had died in the eruption. Around four-fifths of Pompeii's 160 acres (about 65 ha) have been uncovered.

THE ROMAN WRITER PLINY THE YOUNGER WITNESSED THE DRAMATIC ERUPTION:

The cloud was rising from a mountain—at such a distance we couldn't tell which, but afterwards learned that it was Vesuvius. I can best describe its shape by likening it to an umbrella pine tree, with a very tall "trunk" rising high into the sky and then spreading out into "branches." I imagine it had been raised up by the force of the blast, which then weakened, leaving the cloud unsupported so that its own weight caused it to spread sideways. Some of the cloud was white, in other parts it was dark and dirty, as if it carried up earth and cinders.

PLINY THE YOUNGER, *LETTERS* VI, 16

SEE ALSO
• Roman Republic and Empire

616 P o m p e i i

Pottery

Pottery is one of the oldest art forms in the world. As far back as 25,000 BCE people in Europe were making clay figures to use in religious rituals and to give them protection from evil spirits. By the end of the second millennium BCE, the ancient Peruvians in South America were molding clay into jugs, probably to hold liquids for use in rituals.

As people throughout the world changed from hunter-gatherers to farmers, they needed clay pots to store food and drink and to transport it safely from one place to another. In Japan around 10,000 BCE, people were baking clay pots on open fires to make them waterproof. Fragments of pottery found in Turkey show that, by 9000 BCE, people in the eastern Mediterranean were making crude pots for everyday use.

Firing Pottery

By 7500 BCE pottery was in widespread use in China, Africa, and western Asia. Potters formed their wares by hand, often coiling ropes of clay on top of each other to build sturdy pots. The vessels were then left out in the sun to harden. By 6500 BCE most potters in the ancient world were strengthening clay by placing it on a fire. Around 4000 BCE the kiln (a large oven for pottery) came into use in Mesopotamia (present-day Iraq).

The Color of Pottery

Natural pottery is dark red or brown in color. The tint comes from the iron found in most clays, which rusts when it is heated during the pottery-making process.

The Babylonians experimented with various shades of brown to decorate their pottery. Remains found in Susa, in present-day southwest Iran, are decorated with finely drawn geometric patterns, representing birds or dogs. They were made around 3200 BCE.

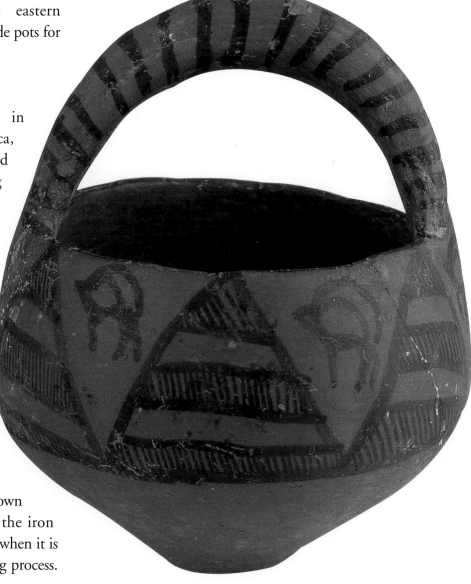

▼ An Iranian potter made this simple vessel some time in the middle of the fifth millennium BCE. It was discovered by archaeologists in what is now Qazvin.

Later the Babylonians covered their pots with copper ore before firing them. When it melted, it produced a deep-blue glaze, which looked very much like lapis lazuli, a semiprecious stone highly prized by the Mesopotamians.

Egyptian Pottery

The Egyptians were producing handmade pottery as early as 3500 BCE. They often placed their red clay pots in hot ashes to blacken the rims (to make a type of pottery known as black-topped ware). Later Egyptian pots were decorated with geometric patterns and also with animals and human figures, painted in white on red pottery. Around 2600 BCE the Egyptians began to use a simple potter's wheel to make fine pots, jars for storing food, and bowls and plates for use at home or in temples. These items were sometimes given a bright blue glazed effect known as faience.

Greek Pottery

By 1500 BCE the Greeks were using glazes that gave their work a rich green or a light blue color. The finest pottery of this period came from the island of Crete, where potters made vases, storage jars known as *pithoi*, and cups as fragile as eggshells. At first these pieces were decorated with abstract designs suggesting plants and animals; later pieces had vivid pictures of mythical heroes, fish, dolphins, starfish hiding in seaweed, and even giant octopuses seemingly gripping the vases themselves.

▶ *This limestone statue of an Egyptian potter at his wheel was put in a grave as an offering during the Fifth Dynasty, which lasted from 2494 to 2435 BCE.*

Between 800 and 300 BCE Greek potters were producing vases known throughout the ancient world for their elegant shape and exquisite decoration. From around 600 BCE Athenian potters started decorating their vases and jugs with human figures in various scenes, often drawn in black against a light background. From 530 BCE the figures were drawn in red. This color allowed the artists to draw figures that looked more realistic, with natural sunburned skin tones. Around 500 BCE potters stopped drawing mere outlines and started painting scenes from various angles. By this time Athenian pottery was so famous that potters started to sign their work.

Roman Pottery

The ancient Romans held Greek pottery in high esteem, importing it to Rome for the use of wealthy Roman citizens. Roman potters were also very skillful. Their most prized pottery was commonly known as Samian ware. It was made in the region of Arretium, present-day Arezzo in Italy. As well as domestic ware, Roman potters produced molded terra-cotta plaques to decorate homes; the plaques often featured scenes from Greek and Roman mythology. Clay lamps, manufactured by the thousand for use in homes and temples, were decorated with simple motifs and sometimes scenes of gladiators fighting. Later ones were embellished with early Christian symbols. Modern versions of these ancient lamps are still used in some churches.

SEE ALSO

- Archaeology • Art • Death and Burial
- Food and Drink • Houses and Homes
- Minoans • Tombs

AMPHORAE

Probably invented in Mycenae, Greece, in the fourteenth century BCE, the amphora was a special vessel used to carry wine, olives, oil, and cereals in ships that traveled the Mediterranean Sea. Made to lie on its side or stand in sand, a typical amphora had a bottom that continued down to a point. Most amphorae were around four and a half feet (1.5 m) in height, though smaller ones were made for use in the home and bigger ones were produced to serve as grave markers.

▼ The makers of this jar, who lived in Knossos on Crete in the late Minoan period (1450–1400 BCE), decorated it with an octopus. The long, swirling tentacles suggest that the artists were trying to portray a giant sea monster.

Prehistory

*P*rehistory is a term used to describe the longest period in human existence. It stretches from the appearance on earth of man's first ancestor, some 2.2 million years ago, to the invention of writing around 3300 BCE. As people in prehistory left no written records, knowledge of prehistoric times depends entirely on archaeological evidence—the ruins of cities, houses, and temples and grave goods.

Homo Habilis

Prehistory begins with the emergence of the members of the earliest form of the human species, known as *Homo habilis*. These early humans lived in the East African grasslands between 2.2 and 1.6 million years ago. Their brain was larger than that of their ancestors, the apelike *Australopithecus Africanus*, who roamed the earth at the same time but who had first appeared much earlier. Being a hunter, *Homo habilis* developed

certain skills that his ancestors did not possess, including muscle coordination and aggressive behavior in the face of danger.

Skulls found in Africa indicate that the *Homo habilis* males were larger than the females. The grassland where they lived was dry and parched and filled with predators, such as leopards and lions. *Homo habilis*, however, was the deadliest predator of all. He made simple stone tools and weapons, which he used to butcher and skin animals,

◀ *Archaeologists found this fractured skull of* Homo habilis *in Lake Turkana in East Africa.*

particularly smaller animals and birds that could be stalked and killed easily.

With the dexterity of *Homo habilis* began the first of three phases in the Stone Age, known as the Paleolithic, or Old Stone Age, a time when people used tools and weapons made of stone. At first *Homo habilis*'s tools were nothing more than chipped stones and pebbles, but by around 100,000 years ago, primitive people were using chisels and pointed axes.

Homo Sapiens Sapiens

The earliest modern humans were members of *Homo sapiens sapiens*. Evidence from skulls and bone fragments suggests that they first appeared around 130,000 years ago. From East Africa they gradually spread to western Asia and by about 35,000 BCE had colonized most of Europe.

Homo sapiens sapiens was the first human to use tools for specific purposes, such as needles made from bones for sewing and harpoons to catch fish. These humans were also the first to express themselves artistically; they left behind many

cave paintings. They showed their sense of spirituality by sacrificing animals and burying their dead in graves.

The First Farmers

By 10,000 BCE many peoples had turned from hunting and gathering food to farming. An early form of wheat was grown in the area now known as the Fertile Crescent, in western Asia. This huge tract of land extended from modern-day Israel to the Persian Gulf and included the Tigris and Euphrates Rivers in Mesopotamia.

▲ *The roughness of these flint tools suggests that they were made and used during the Upper Paleolithic period, which lasted from 35,000 to 10,000 BCE.*

THE ICE AGE

Homo sapiens sapiens *developed during an ice age that ended around 13,000 BCE. As the world's climate warmed and the ice sheets melted, people spread farther and wider around the world. Communities were established in many places, including China, Mexico, and Peru. The stone tools used during the Ice Age were adapted to the new conditions.*

The end of the Ice Age marks the start of the second phase of the Stone Age, known as the Mesolithic period, or Middle Stone Age. In the relatively advanced cultures of western and Southeast Asia, the Stone Age lasted until around 6000 BCE. In other parts of the world, including the Americas, it persisted until 2500 BCE or even later.

Around 9750 BCE, the first pottery was being made in Japan. Farmers in Thailand started growing peas, beans, and water chestnuts.

People in the Andes Mountains and in western Asia were also beginning to experiment with farming around 8000 BCE. This third and last phase of the Stone Age is known as the Neolithic period, or New Stone Age. During this period stone tools became more varied and sophisticated, stone knives were given handles, and farmers started using stone hoes to break up the soil in their fields.

By 7000 BCE potatoes and other root crops were being grown in the Andes, while farmers in the Amazon were cultivating manioc and people in Mexico were eating squash, beans, and chili peppers. In Libya, Egypt, and Algeria the first shepherds were tending their flocks. By 6000 BCE people in southern Europe and India had also taken up farming, and Chinese farmers were domesticating animals.

Early Communities

Up until the eighth millennium BCE, people in western Asia had been nomads, wandering around the land in search of food. When they started farming, however, they stayed in one place to look after the crops. They also had to defend their land from others who wanted their harvest. The same pattern of behavior appeared in Europe some time in the sixth millennium BCE, in East Asia during the fourth millennium, and in sub-Saharan Africa during the third. As dependency on crops grew stronger, it became essential for people to band together in bigger, more stable communities. Small villages grew into the world's first towns.

▶ By the fifth millennium BCE people had started to make tools and weapons out of polished stone. Implements such as these axes and hammers have been found in many places around Europe, including Austria, Hungary, and, as with these examples, the Czech Republic.

THE ARRIVAL OF WRITING

As early as 8000 BCE, when the first city developed in Sumer, Sumerian people recorded simple calculations by making indentations on clay. The calculations became increasingly complex, and by around 3300 BCE, the accounting system had evolved into a full writing system, known as cuneiform. Literally, cuneiform means "wedge-shaped" and refers to the shapes made by a stylus (usually a reed) on clay tablets. The development of cuneiform writing marks the end of prehistory in Sumer.

It had long been thought that cuneiform was the world's first writing system and that the Egyptians based their system of hieroglyphs on what they learned from the Sumerians. However, discoveries made at Abydos in southern Egypt in 1988 suggest that the Egyptians were using hieroglyphs aound 3250 BCE, at the same time as the Sumerians were developing cuneiform. It also seems that the Egyptians invented their complex system from scratch.

In China prehistory ended with the invention of a system of writing around 1500 BCE. In other places prehistory survived longer, until the art of writing spread to most parts of the world. Written documents have afforded historians an unmatched window on the past.

▲ This Sumerian clay tablet, inscribed with cuneiform writing, dates to around 2000 BCE, when the great civilization of ancient Sumer was entering its final phase.

It was essential for these early communities to appoint leaders who could organize them into an efficient workforce. These leaders allocated different tasks to their workers, managed irrigation projects, oversaw the harvest, and paid the skilled workers who supplied the village with tools and implements. This organization was an early form of government and a major step toward modern civilization.

Around 6000 BCE copper was used for the first time in western Asia. The Stone Age had come to an end in the Fertile Crescent and Southeast Asia but continued in Europe, the rest of Asia, and Africa until around 4000 BCE.

SEE ALSO
• Egypt • Farming
• Hunting and Fishing
• Sumer • Writing

Ptolemy

Claudius Ptolemy was a Greek astronomer, mathematician, and geographer. Born in Egypt in about 85 CE, he lived and worked in Alexandria and died around 165. He evidently came from a Greek family living in Egypt and was probably a Roman citizen.

▼ In this fifteenth-century-CE painting, Ptolemy contemplates an armillary sphere. The device, which Ptolemy himself invented, shows the position of important planets and stars in the celestial sphere, which Ptolemy believed surrounded the earth.

The dates of Ptolemy's first and last astronomical observations are March 26, 127 CE, and February 2, 141. Otherwise, very little is known about Ptolemy's life, though he refers in his writings to teachers who influenced him, including Theon the Mathematician, from Smyrna in Asia Minor, and someone named Syrus.

Astronomical Work

In mapping many new stars, Ptolemy increased the Greek astronomer Hipparchus's count of 850 to 1,022. He devised the astrolabe, an instrument used to measure the geometrical height above the horizon of stars and planets. He also invented a rough system of measuring star brightness by "magnitude." The brightest stars were first magnitude, the faintest were sixth. From his observations, he compiled so-called Handy Tables, which supplied details of the future positions of the sun, moon, stars, and planets, including times when eclipses would occur.

The *Almagest*

Ptolemy's best-known work is the thirteen-volume *Almagest* (its Latin name; in Arabic, *al-majisti,* and in Greek, *he megiste*). The title means "the greatest compilation."

In the *Almagest* Ptolemy collected, revised, and improved on the views of earlier Greek astronomers, notably Hipparchus. Greek astronomers believed that the earth stayed motionless at the center of the universe and that the sun, stars, and planets revolved round it. Only Aristarchos of Samos, who lived around 275 BCE, said that the earth, stars, and planets revolved around the sun, but he was not believed.

The Ptolemaic System

This earth-at-the-center view of the universe was called the Ptolemaic system, after Ptolemy. According to the Ptolemaic system, the sun, moon, and planets moved in a circular path because they were fixed

This illustrated page showing Ptolemy's world-view, with the earth at the center of the universe and the other planets orbiting around it, comes from a book published as late as 1660.

within revolving, invisible spheres of crystal. Each crystalline sphere nested inside a larger one—a glass onion, as it were. Pythagoras suggested that their movement made "heavenly music," which could not be heard by humans.

The Greeks had long puzzled over the "wandering" movements of five planets: Mercury, Mars, Jupiter, Venus, and Saturn. (The Greek word *planetai* means "wanderers.") Ptolemy's mathematics helped to demonstrate how the planets wandered in spheres that circled within other, larger revolving spheres.

The *Guide to Geography* and Other Works

Ptolemy's *Guide to Geography* contained ideas for fixing lines of latitude (imaginary lines that circle the earth parallel to the equator) and longitude (lines that run from Pole to Pole). It also contained instructions for making maps, with details—sometimes wrong—of where places were located. Later mapmakers drew up misleading charts based on his ideas. Ptolemy also wrote on musical theory, in *Harmonica*, and on light, in *Optics*. He even wrote horoscopes and built sundials.

PTOLEMY WROTE THE FOLLOWING SHORT POEM:

I know very well that I am mortal, a creature of a day.
But when my mind follows the winding paths of the stars,
My feet are not confined to the earth—
I stand next to Zeus himself, and take my fill
of the food of the gods, ambrosia.

PTOLEMY, ALMAGEST, BOOK 1

SEE ALSO
- Alexandria
- Astronomy
- Egypt
- Geography
- Greek Philosophy

Pyramids

Several civilizations built pyramids. Made from stone, brick, rubble, or compacted soil, they usually had square bases and four steep sides, which were either smooth or rose up in a series of steps, or platforms. The sides of some, such as those of the ancient Egyptians, met at a point at the top. Pyramids built by other cultures, especially those of the Americas, had flat tops. Small pyramids have also been found on the Canary Islands, off the northwest coast of Africa.

Pyramids of the Egyptians

The pyramids of ancient Egypt were royal tombs. They evolved from mastaba tombs, first made in around 3100 BCE. A mastaba was made from mud bricks piled into a low, flat-topped, rectangular mound. Beneath it was a burial chamber.

During the reign of Djoser, which lasted from 2667 to 2648 BCE, the architect Imhotep built his master a large mastaba tomb. Imhotep used stone, not mud brick. On top of the stone mastaba, he added a smaller stone platform and a smaller one on top of that. Eventually the stone mound rose up in six steps. It was ancient Egypt's first pyramid. Because of its shape, it is known as the Step Pyramid.

In the reign of Sneferu, from 2613 to 2589 BCE, the first smooth-sided, or true, pyramid was built. Sneferu's son Khufu, (reigned 2589–2566 BCE) created the largest of all pyramids, at Giza, near present-day Cairo. Called the Great Pyramid, it rises 481 feet (146 m) and is made from 2.3 million blocks of stone. About a hundred pyramids were built in Egypt between about 2650 and 1550 BCE, but tomb robbers broke into them. Thus, from around 1550 BCE, Egypt's pharaohs were buried in rock-cut tombs, and no more pyramids were built in Egypt. Between 750 BCE and 350 CE, at the end of ancient Egyptian history, about 180 small pyramids were built in Nubia (present-day Sudan) by the Kushite pharaohs, who at one time had also ruled Egypt.

Pyramids of the Americas

In a desert valley in Peru lies the ancient city of Caral. In 2001 archaeologists obtained a radiocarbon date of 2627 BCE for the city and thus concluded that Caral's six pyra-

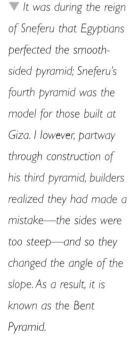

It was during the reign of Sneferu that Egyptians perfected the smooth-sided pyramid; Sneferu's fourth pyramid was the model for those built at Giza. However, partway through construction of his third pyramid, builders realized they had made a mistake—the sides were too steep—and so they changed the angle of the slope. As a result, it is known as the Bent Pyramid.

mids had been built at the same time as those at Giza. Caral's flat-topped platform pyramids, the biggest of which stands 65 feet (20 m) high, were built with stone walls filled in with rubble and rock.

In Mesoamerica (Mexico and Central America) pyramids were built from 1000 BCE until the Spanish conquest in the sixteenth century CE. The earliest, in the Mexican state of Tabasco, dates from between 1000 and 400 BCE. It was built by the Olmecs, from beaten soil faced with (that is, covered with a layer of) clay.

AMERICAN PYRAMID EXPLORER

Born in Indianapolis, Indiana, George Andrew Reisner (1867–1942) was an Egyptologist noted for high standards of excavation. He recognized the importance of photography and used it to document his discoveries. From 1899 to 1905 he excavated pyramids at Giza. His most important discovery was the rock-cut tomb of Queen Hetepheres, wife of Sneferu. In Nubia (present-day southern Egypt and northern Sudan) he found the pyramid tombs of seventy-three Nubian rulers, some of them dating to the eighth century BCE.

◀ Around 145 feet (44 m) tall, the Temple of the Giant Jaguar, at Tikal, Guatemala, built between 600 and 900 CE, is one of the most impressive of all Mayan temple pyramids.

MESOPOTAMIAN ZIGGURATS

Between around 2200 and 550 BCE pyramid structures were built in Mesopotamia (an area in modern Iraq and also parts of Iran, Turkey, and Syria). Known as ziggurats, from the Akkadian word ziqqurratu, meaning "to build high," these pyramid-shaped temple towers were a center of religious life and were common to the Sumerians, Babylonians, and Assyrians. A ziggurat was thought of as a "ladder" linking heaven and earth. It rose up in a series of mud-brick platforms from a rectangular, oval, or square base. Some of the outer bricks were glazed in bright colors. The platforms were reached by ramps and staircases. At the top were one or more temples.

▼ At its peak, between 450 and 650 CE, Teotihuacán, Mexico, was one of the ancient world's largest cities, with a population of 150,000. The massive Pyramid of the Sun dominated the city center.

At the city of Teotihuacán, Mexico, is the Pyramid of the Sun, built between 1 and 250 CE. Formed from five platforms, it is made from rubble faced with cobblestones. It stands on a square base, and its original height was about 200 feet (61 m).

Pyramids built by the Maya are found from Mexico to El Salvador. The earliest are at El Mirador, Guatemala, where the Danta Pyramid, at 230 feet (70 m), is the tallest structure the Maya ever built. These pyramids date from 200 BCE to 150 CE. The Maya built pyramids, from stone blocks sealed with lime mortar, until around 1000 CE.

Unlike the pyramids of Egypt, the pyramids of the Americas were not tombs. Instead, they were the central structures in a complex of other buildings. On their flat tops were shrines, where priests performed religious duties. Stairways led from the ground to the top.

SEE ALSO

• Assyrians • Egypt
• Maya
• Mesopotamia
• Nubians
• Olmecs
• Teotihuacán

Pythagoras

The Greek mathematician Pythagoras lived on the island of Samos between about 569 and 475 BCE. Also a philosopher and religious teacher, he influenced later philosophers, particularly Plato.

Although none of Pythagoras's writings have survived, works exist by ancient writers, known as Pythagoreans, that claim to give Pythagoras's views and sometimes his very words. These early accounts, which tend to blend fact and legend, present him as a godlike figure.

Early Life

Pythagoras was taken by his father, a merchant, to Italy and Syria. He was taught in both places for a while but was educated mainly in Samos, where he learned to play the lyre and to recite Homer's epic poems. He was introduced to mathematical ideas by Thales, who lived on Miletus, and Anaximander, who lectured there.

In 535 BCE Pythagoras apparently went to Egypt and became a priest at a temple in Diapolis. As a priest he abstained from eating beans and wearing clothing made from animals and took vows of secrecy. Later he may have been taken to Babylon as a prisoner of war and perhaps remained there as a student.

Later Teaching

About 520 BCE Pythagoras returned to Samos and founded a school. In 518 he left Samos for Croton, a Greek colony in southeast Italy. There he founded another school, where his followers lived communally as vegetarians and without personal possessions.

This secretive society adopted Pythagorean ideas, particularly the belief that "the whole cosmos is a scale and a number." Pythagoras came to this conclusion by observing strings on musical instruments. He noticed that those that vibrated in harmony with one another were related mathematically through the ratios of their lengths.

▼ This sculpted head of Pythagoras is a Roman copy of a lost Greek original.

Pythagoras and his followers established various theorems. The most famous of them showed that the square based on the hypotenuse of a right-angled triangle (one having one 90° angle) equaled the sum of the squares based on the other two sides. Another said that the sum of the angles of a triangle equaled two right angles.

▼ *An Arab scribe copied this page from Pythagoras's* Elements *in about 1200 CE.*

Belief and Persecution

Acccording to Pythagoras's key religious belief, after death, the soul migrates from one creature to another. He is supposed to have stopped someone from beating a small dog, saying, "Stop . . . for it is the soul of a dear friend—I recognized it when I heard the voice." This belief may also explain why he abstained from meat and followed a vegetarian diet.

The Pythagoreans' society in Croton was attacked, perhaps around 508 BCE, and Pythagoras fled to Metapontum nearby, where he is supposed to have committed suicide. Some say, though, that he came back to Croton and lived to be a hundred. His work lived on through various Pythagorean societies, which survived until about 400 CE.

THE WRITER APOLLONIUS MENTIONS SEVERAL LEGENDS THAT CREDITED PYTHAGORAS WITH HAVING MAGICAL POWERS:

Once he appeared both in Croton and Metapontum on the same day and at the very same time. On another occasion, when he was sitting in the theater, he stood up, so Aristotle says, and revealed to the audience around him that his thigh was made of gold.

APOLLONIUS, MARVELOUS STORIES

SEE ALSO

- Babylon • Egypt • Greek Philosophy
- Music and Dance • Numbers • Plato

Ramayana

The *Ramayana* is the shorter of India's two ancient epic poems, just a quarter of the length of the *Mahabharata*. Unlike the longer poem, it is believed to be largely the work of a single author, Valmiki, about whose life nothing is known. The *Ramayana* is thought to date from between 200 BCE and 200 CE.

The *Ramayana* tells the story of Rama, king of Ayodhya in northern India. Like Krishna in the *Mahabharata*, he is an avatar, or earthly form, of the great god Vishnu, who comes down from heaven whenever the world needs him. Vishnu takes on the form of Rama in order to destroy a wicked demon named Ravana.

In the poem Rama is the perfect hero, handsome, brave, virtuous, and clever. Unlike Arjuna, the hero of the *Mahabharata*, he never has any doubts about where his duty lies. The heroine is Rama's equally perfect wife, Sita, who is beautiful and wholly devoted to her husband.

Rama's enemy is Ravana, a demon king with ten heads. Ravana kidnaps Sita and takes her to his island kingdom of Lanka (probably Sri Lanka), where he tries to persuade her to become his wife. Sita refuses, thinking only of her beloved husband.

The Search for Sita

Rama searches desperately for his wife. He is helped by the monkey king, Hanuman, who sends his army of monkeys out on the quest. After growing to a huge size and leaping across the sea to Lanka, Hanuman eventually finds Sita. He comforts her and then returns to Rama to tell him the good news.

▶ *An eighth-century-CE carving of Hanuman, the helpful monkey king.*

Overjoyed, Rama rushes to the coast, where the monkeys build a bridge to the island out of trees and rocks. Rama and his monkey army cross over and fight a great battle with Ravana and his demons. There is hard-fought combat between the rival kings, each riding a chariot. Rama, firing arrow after arrow, cuts down Ravana's ten heads, but the demon keeps growing new ones. Eventually Rama kills him by shooting a sacred dart into his chest.

The Popularity of the *Ramayana*

The *Ramayana* is one of the most important Hindu texts dealing with ethics (correct moral behavior). It is still one of the most popular stories in India, and it has been translated from its original Sanskrit into most of the other Indian languages. The story is recited by traveling performers and reenacted in puppet shows and dances. It has inspired films, television dramatizations, paintings, and comic books. The hero, Rama, is worshiped as a god in Hindu temples, and each October and November, his homecoming with Sita is celebrated by millions of Hindus during Diwali, the festival of lights.

▼ The demon Ravana glares at the hero, Rama, and his brother, Lakshmana.

WATCHING FROM HEAVEN, THE GODS CELEBRATE THE DEATH OF THE DEMON RAVANA. VISHNU'S PURPOSE IN TAKING HUMAN FORM, AS RAMA, HAS BEEN FULFILLED:

From heaven, flowers rained down upon the blood-soaked plain,
And unseen instruments played lovely melodies.
The ocean swelled with happiness, the sun shone more brightly,
And soft breezes blew sweet scents from the trees.
Then a voice of blessing came down from the bright sky,
"Champion of the true, the righteous! Now your noble task is done!"

RAMAYANA

SEE ALSO
• Hinduism
• Indian Philosophy
• Mahabharata

Ramses II

Ramses II ruled Egypt from 1279 BCE to 1213 BCE. He was about twenty-five years old when he became pharaoh, and he ruled for sixty-six years. Seven different pharaohs had ruled in the previous forty-five years. Ramses' long reign therefore brought stability to Egypt.

Making Egypt Safe

Egypt was under continual threat from its neighbors in times of change and upheaval, such as that preceding Ramses' reign. Upon becoming pharaoh, Ramses raised a huge army, numbering over 20,000 soldiers, and went to war with the Hittites. The war ended with both sides claiming victory but with the Hittites promising not to attack Egypt. Though Ramses used warfare to secure Egypt's borders, he also married princesses from other lands as part of peace agreements. His wives included Hittite, Syrian, and Babylonian princesses.

Building a Family

Some of the previous pharaohs had not had enough children to have a clear male successor. To ensure that he had plenty of heirs, Ramses married at least eight royal wives, of whom the most important was Nefertari. He also had many other, lesser wives. By the time of his death, he had over a hundred children. Although twelve of his sons died before their father, there were still enough left to be sure of a successor.

Building a Reputation

During his long reign Ramses II had many temples built. The most famous of these is the temple at Abu Simbel, with its huge statues of Ramses himself. He built other temples all along the Nile River, from the delta to Nubia (present-day southern Egypt and northern Sudan). He reused many of his predecessors' statues and temples as part of his building work. He also built a grand new city named Piramesse in the Nile Delta.

▼ The head of one of the colossal statues of Ramses II at Abu Simbel.

RAMSES II AND THE BIBLE

Some historians believe that Ramses II is the pharaoh in the biblical story of the Israelites' flight from Egypt. According to the Book of Exodus, the Israelites had been slaves in Egypt for over four hundred years when God took pity on them and told one of them, Moses, to go to the pharaoh and demand freedom for his people. Ten times Moses went to the pharaoh, and ten times the pharaoh refused to let the Israelites go. After each refusal, God sent a plague upon Egypt; one was crop-eating locusts, another was frogs, and another was painful boils. The tenth plague was the death of the first-born child of every Egyptian, including the pharaoh's eldest son. The pharaoh, beginning to fear the Israelites and their God, said the Israelites could go. Once they had gone, however, the pharaoh regretted losing so many slaves—a total of about six thousand men and their families—so he sent a huge army to bring them back into slavery.

The Israelites had just reached the Red Sea when they heard the Egyptian army behind them. Trapped, they cried out to God, who told them to go on. Moses was in front, his staff stretched out over the water. As they walked, the waters of the Red Sea parted, and the Israelites were thus able to cross on dry ground, a huge wall of water welled up on either side of them. However, when the Egyptians tried to follow, the walls of water came crashing down, and they drowned.

▲ This statue of Ramses II stands in the Great Temple of Amun at Karnak, in Luxor, Egypt.

SEE ALSO

- Egypt • Hebrews
- Moses

Religion

Religion has existed for as long as humans have sought to understand whether human life has deeper purposes. As long as 100,000 years ago, primitive people buried their dead in marked graves, together with tools, weapons, and animal bones, an indication that these people believed that life continued, in some form, after death. Experts have yet to discover an ancient civilization that was nonreligious. Although beliefs and methods of worship differed, people of every civilization in the ancient world asked questions—and provided similar answers—about the force or forces that created and controlled the world.

The Earliest Idea of God

By 15,000 BCE people were drawing images on cave walls. These caves were not dwellings; some experts believe they were seen as places where people could commune with higher beings. The remarkable cave paintings discovered in Lascaux in France in 1940 show one of these higher beings, a shadowy figure who is half human and half stag. Other figures in the cave, hunters in masks, suggest that the drawers saw a connection between the hunters and an invisible, magical world.

By 4000 BCE the idea of supernatural beings controlling the natural world had taken root and strengthened. A carved soapstone seal found in Mohenjo Daro, in the Indus valley, shows a holy being sitting cross-legged in thought, an early form of the god that would one day be known as Shiva, one of the three most important gods of Hinduism.

◀ This famous soapstone seal, made between 2300 and 1750 BCE, shows a sacred entity meditating. One of many seals found in Mohenjo Daro on the banks of the Indus River, it affords a rare glimpse into the religious life of the ancient Harappan civilization.

Sumerian Religion

By 2250 BCE the people of ancient Sumer had a pantheon (a collection of gods). Each god represented one or more elements of nature. The Sumerians had a god of the air, a god of the sea, a god of the plow, and a goddess of love and war.

The Sumerians' religion was far more advanced than those of other ancient peoples. They spent more public money than any other nation of the time on building temples, called ziggurats. The sacrifices they made to their gods included offering the blood of people and animals.

▶ *This statue of the Persian god Mithras slaying a bull was made by an Athenian carver in the second century CE. Bull sacrifice was an important ceremony in Mithraism, a popular religious cult of the Roman Empire.*

The Sumerians believed that they had been created to serve the gods and that when they died, they went to a gloomy underworld, where everyone was sad for all eternity. Their religious festivals enacted the story of creation, one of the first attempts by human beings to explain their origin. The king was seen as the high priest of the country. He was surrounded by priests, who were respected and feared by the people because they were thought to possess magical powers.

Ancient Egyptian Religion

The ancient Egyptians also believed that religion, magic, and nature were linked. Religion pervaded every aspect of Egyptian life. It has been estimated that there were over one thousand Egyptian gods. In the early stages of Egyptian civilization, many gods were animal deities; they symbolized different aspects of the natural world.

As Egyptian society became more sophisticated, its gods took on more humanlike qualities. One of the Egyptians' most beloved goddesses was Isis, who was revered as a mother figure. By Egypt's late period (around 750 BCE) Isis had taken on many of the qualities of Hathor, who was the goddess of love.

Egyptians worried about what would happen to their soul after death. One of the main concerns of their religion was preparation for the afterlife.

Ancient Greek Religion

Like the Egyptians, the Greeks had many gods. Their gods were thought to reside on Mount Olympus, from where they watched the lives of ordinary mortals. The ancient Greeks felt that life had to be lived by a set of rules. Those people who disobeyed the rules met with the disapproval and anger of

THE MOTHER GODDESS

Around 3500 BCE people in the Mediterranean and western Asia were worshiping a female goddess of fertility. Clay figurines found on the island of Malta show a big-hipped mother goddess. She would later be worshiped under many different names: Inanna in Sumer, Isis and Hathor in Egypt, and Aphrodite in ancient Greece.

the gods (this disapproval was personified as as Nemesis). Greek religion was a mixture of myths and superstitions based on stories of the gods. People joined cults that performed strange rituals, they offered sacrifices to please the deities, and they consulted diviners who foretold what the gods had planned for their future. Unlike the gods of Babylon and Egypt, on whom they were based, the Greek gods showed human emotions as well as godlike behavior.

Ancient Roman Religion

The ancient Romans inherited the gods and many of the religious ideas of the Greeks. The main Roman god was Jupiter, based on the Greek Zeus. Other deities included Dionysus, the god of wine (whom the Greeks worshiped as Bacchus), and Minerva, the goddess of wisdom (based on the Greek Athena).

As the Roman Empire spread around and beyond the Mediterranean, people started worshiping gods from conquered countries. For example, Mithras, a Persian god, was the favorite deity of Roman soldiers. His was a "men-only" religion whose followers sacrificed bulls. Another favorite was the Egyptian Isis, whose worship spread as far as Britain under Roman occupation.

◀ Made out of glassy blue faience sometime between 664 and 525 BCE, this statue shows the Egyptian goddess Isis sitting on a throne with her son, the infant god Horus, on her lap.

HOLY SCRIPTURES

*A*lmost all religions have sacred scriptures, holy writings that are believed to be inspired in some measure by God or the gods. Buddhist sacred writings tell of the life of Gautama Buddha and his teachings in the sixth century BCE. The oldest scripture of the Indo-European world is the Rig-Veda, part of the sacred writings of Hinduism. A collection of hymns describing creation and the life of gods such as Shiva and Vishnu, the Rig-Veda dates from around 1500 BCE.

The Jewish scriptures, called the Old Testament by Christians, were selected from a bigger body of sacred literature in 90 CE. Jesus left none of his own writings, but four of his followers were inspired to write about his life. Their books, known as the Gospels, now form part of the New Testament.

▼ Part of a marble sarcophagus made for a Roman prefect named Junius Bassus, this carving shows the prophet Abraham about to demonstrate his love for God by sacrificing his son Isaac.

Judaism and Christianity

Around 2000 BCE a Hebrew nomad named Abraham embraced the idea of worshiping only one deity. This event marked the first time in history that people believed in one, all-encompassing god.

In 6 CE, at the height of the Roman Empire, Jesus was born in Palestine. The teachings Jesus added to the old Jewish scriptures became the foundation of the New Testament of the Christian Bible. After Jesus was crucified, his followers spread his faith around the Roman world. The new religion spoke of a life based on love and compassion, of resurrection, and of an eternal life with God in heaven. By 380 CE Emperor Theodosius had forbidden the worship of the ancient gods. Before long, Christianity would become the most influential religion in the Western world.

SEE ALSO
- Buddhism • Christianity
- Egyptian Mythology • Greek Mythology
- Hinduism • Judaism • Mythology • Women

Glossary

abacus A frame holding wires on which beads can be moved, used for counting and calculating.

ambrosia Food of the gods.

aqueduct A stone channel, raised on walls, columns, or arches, designed to carry water across a valley.

blasphemy The sin of acting or speaking in a way disrespectful to God.

caravan A column of merchants traveling, usually on camels, across desert country.

cella The most sacred part of a temple or shrine, often containing the cult statue.

circumcision The Jewish custom of removing the foreskin from the penis of a baby boy.

delta An area of wet, marshy land formed by a river that breaks into several parts as it joins the sea.

forum The town square in the middle of a Roman town, used for markets, political meetings, and processions.

gild Cover with gold leaf.

glaze A shiny coating on pottery.

Hellenistic period The period of Greek civilization between the late fourth and first centuries BCE.

hieroglyph Symbol in a system of picture writing used by the Egyptians, the Maya, and other ancient civilizations. Individual hieroglyphs could stand for objects, concepts, or sounds.

Hittite A member of a people who lived in the land between the Mediterranean and the Black Seas; at their most powerful the Hittites controlled an empire that reached down into Syria.

irrigation A method of bringing a supply of water to dry land, especially to help crops grow.

kaolin Fine white clay used in pottery and paper making.

latitude An imaginary straight line around the earth parallel to the equator.

Levant The eastern shore of the Mediterranean, from Greece to Egypt.

longitude An imaginary straight line around the earth from the North to the South Pole.

manioc A root vegetable.

myrrh A pleasant-smelling gum obtained from various trees in Africa and southern Asia; it is used in perfume, incense, and medicinal preparations.

obsidian A type of hard, sharp volcanic glass used by many ancient civilizations to make spear tips and cutting tools.

palaestra A square courtyard used for wrestling, weight lifting, and other sports.

pantheon All the gods of a given culture or people.

quoit A ring of metal for throwing.

rabbi In Judaism, a religious leader and teacher.

radiocarbon dating A dating method that relies on the fact that carbon 14, a radioactive isotope present in all living things, decays at a known rate and thus enables fixed points in time to be calculated.

ritual An action or series of actions used in a ceremony, generally religious.

sacred Holy; having to do with God or a god.

Seven Wonders of the World The seven structures that ancient scholars considered to be the most remarkable in the world; they comprise the pyramids of Egypt, the giant bronze statue of the god Apollo in Rhodes, the statue of Zeus at Olympia carved by Phidias, the temple of the goddess Artemis in Ephesus, the lighthouse of Alexandria, the mausoleum of Halicarnassus, and the Hanging Gardens of Babylon.

soapstone A soft rock.

terra-cotta Unglazed reddish-brown hard-baked clay, often used to make pottery objects.

theorem A mathematical statement that can be proved by reasoning.

tribute Payment made by one state or tribe to another as a sign of submission.

votive offering An offering made to the gods in the hope of receiving a blessing or favor in return.

Index

Page numbers in **boldface type** refer to main articles.
Page numbers in *italic type* refer to illustrations.